What Others Are Saying

"God cares about you up close and personal. In 1990, on the 24th of May, my father had a heart attack and died. At his funeral, I felt sad that there had been no real relationship for me to miss him. I prayed that God would show me His love for me as a Father. Fast forward nine years. On the 20th of May this year, God gave Rhema, who I had never met, my name in prayer; and instructed her to pray because the enemy was trying to destroy me.

On the 24th of May I had a stroke. Three hours into the clot busting medication, I had an adverse reaction—a brain hemorrhage. My husband Ernie Culley prayed, God healed, and the doctor was confused. God showed me His great love by giving my name to a faithful woman who I had never met.

We met a few weeks later, and now I have a friend for life; who is faithful to her God, and loves unconditionally. You too can meet her through the pages of this book. But her desire for you is that you meet the One who loves us all—Jesus Christ, Son of God."

Pastor Merrilyn Culley
Vancouver, Canada

"As an author, former academic and diplomat, I have for years failed the challenge to come to Jesus as a child full of wonder and expectation. Several decades ago, I faced a huge family health crisis that was to cost me my diplomatic career, and almost ended my marriage. Jesus rescued me, saved my marriage, now entering its 58th year, and introduced me to seeing the world increasingly as He sees it.

The great Christian author, C. S. Lewis, used the words 'surprised by joy' to describe his Christian conversion. I was surprised by my child-like wonder, and expectation. But, over time, my intellect got in the way and increasingly robbed me of that initial intimacy.

That was my situation when I picked up Rhema's remarkable book. Due to my recent years of struggling with my wife's worsening Alzheimer's, on top of her earlier illnesses, I had developed a rather defensive faith—salvation assured, but not much to expect this side of heaven.

Rhema's world, vividly described in *God Is Concerned About You* is full of expectation and intimate interaction with her Saviour and mine. I was brought back to those days of wonder and, I believe, some of that expectant awe has rubbed off on me.

My prayer is that you too will be similarly blessed by Rhema's words.

Ray Robinson, Executive Chairman
Canadian Environmental Assessment
Ottawa, Canada

God Is Concerned About You

(Second Edition)

By

Rhema Orech

WORLD WIDE
PUBLISHING GROUP

7710-T Cherry Park Dr, Ste 224
Houston, TX 77095
www.WorldwidePublishingGroup.com

Scripture quotations, unless otherwise noted, are from the King James Version of the Holy Bible.

The views expressed in this book are those of the author and do not necessarily reflect those of the publisher.

Published in the United States of America.

Ebook: 978-3-9592-6979-7

Softcover: 978-0692579763

Hardcover: 978-1-60796-888-7

FOREWORD

When God spoke to Abraham in Genesis 12, He told him among other things, that he (Abraham) would be a blessing. Paul tells us, in the Book of Galatians, that we who belong to Jesus Christ will inherit the blessings of Abraham.

We occasionally meet someone who has somehow put it all together; and who walks in the fullness of the reality of that promise. Such a person is Rhema Orech. Sister Rhema impacted our lives powerfully before we ever met her. She has a wonderful ability to hear the voice and instructions of the Holy Spirit; the discernment to understand her assignment; and the self-discipline to carry out each task.

Such an assignment sent her into deep intercessory prayer for my wife, Marrilyn, before either of us ever met her. In the midst of the greatest crisis of our lives, I walked up to Merrilyn, lying on a hospital bed in the Intensive Care Ward at *Vancouver General Hospital*, laid my hands on her head, and said, "Jesus, there's something going on in this head right now. We need a miracle, and we need it now." Today I am convinced that simple prayer unleashed an avalanche of stored up prayer power, and my Merrilyn was instantly, miraculously healed!

Since that initial intervention, we have "done life together" with Rhema Orech, this wonderful woman of God. She continuously proves the reality of that ancient promise to Abraham, and to his descendants. Rhema is a walking blessing of God Himself. In this book, she allows us all to join her on this amazing adventure she calls life.

Pastor Ernie Culley
Vancouver, Canada

Table of Contents

CHAPTER ONE
LOVE IS CONCERNED

God's Creation and Control

¹ *In the beginning God created the heaven and the earth.* ² *And the earth was without form, and void; and darkness was upon the face of the deep. And the Spirit of God moved upon the face of the waters.* ³ *And God said, Let there be light: and there was light.* ⁴ *And God saw the light, that it was good: and God divided the light from the darkness.* ⁵ *And God called the light Day, and the darkness he called Night. And the evening and the morning were the first day.* ⁶ *And God said, Let there be a firmament in the midst of the waters, and let it divide the waters from the waters.* ⁷ *And God made the firmament, and divided the waters which were under the firmament from the waters which were above the firmament: and it was so.* ⁸ *And God called the firmament Heaven. And the evening and the morning were the second day.* ⁹ *And God said, Let the waters under the heaven be gathered together unto one place, and let the dry land appear: and it was so.* ¹⁰ *And God called the dry land Earth; and the gathering together of the waters called he Seas: and God saw that it was good.* ¹¹ *And God said, Let the earth bring forth grass, the herb yielding seed, and the fruit tree yielding fruit after his kind, whose seed is in itself, upon the earth:*

and it was so. ¹² *And the earth brought forth grass, and herb yielding seed after his kind, and the tree yielding fruit, whose seed was in itself, after his kind: and God saw that it was good.* ¹³ *And the evening and the morning were the third day.* ¹⁴ *And God said, Let there be lights in the firmament of the heaven to divide the day from the night; and let them be for signs, and for seasons, and for days, and years:* ¹⁵ *And let them be for lights in the firmament of the heaven to give light upon the earth: and it was so.* ¹⁶ *And God made two great lights; the greater light to rule the day, and the lesser light to rule the night: he made the stars also.* ¹⁷ *And God set them in the firmament of the heaven to give light upon the earth,* ¹⁸ *And to rule over the day and over the night, and to divide the light from the darkness: and God saw that it was good.* ¹⁹ *And the evening and the morning were the fourth day.* ²⁰ *And God said, Let the waters bring forth abundantly the moving creature that hath life, and fowl that may fly above the earth in the open firmament of heaven.* ²¹ *And God created great whales, and every living creature that moveth, which the waters brought forth abundantly, after their kind, and every winged fowl after his kind: and God saw that it was good.* ²² *And God blessed them, saying, be fruitful, and multiply, and fill the waters in the seas, and let fowl multiply in the earth.* ²³ *And the evening and the morning were the fifth day.* ²⁴ *And God said, Let the earth bring forth the living creature after his kind, cattle, and creeping thing, and beast of the earth* after his kind: and it was so. ²⁵ And God made the beast of the earth after his kind, and cattle after their kind, and every thing that creepeth upon the earth after his kind: and God saw that it was good. ²⁶ And God said, Let us make man in our image, after our likeness: and let them have dominion over the fish of the sea, and over the fowl of the air, and over the cattle, and over all the earth, and over every creeping thing that creepeth upon the earth. ²⁷ So God created man in his own image, in the image of God created he him; male and female created he them. ²⁸ And God blessed them, and God said unto them, Be fruitful, and multiply, and replenish the earth, and subdue it: and have dominion over the fish of the sea, and over the fowl of the air, and over every living thing that moveth upon the earth. ²⁹ And God said, Behold, I have given you every herb bearing seed, which is upon the face of all the earth, and every tree, in the which is the fruit of a tree yielding seed; to you it shall be for meat. ³⁰ And to every beast of the earth, and to every fowl of the air, and to every thing that creepeth upon the earth, wherein there is life, I have given every green herb for meat: and it was so. ³¹ And God saw every thing that he had made, and, behold, it was very good. And the evening and the morning were the sixth day" (Genesis 1:1-31).

God's word is true. When He speaks, all doubts vanish because:

"... the word of God is quick, and powerful, and sharper than any two-edged sword, piercing even to the dividing asunder of soul and spirit, and of the joints and marrow, and is a discerner of the thoughts and intents of the heart" (Hebrews 4:12).

"In the beginning was the Word, and the Word was with God, and the Word was God. The same was in the beginning with God. All things were made by him; and without him was not any thing made that was made" (John 1: 1-3).

"Thou art worthy, O Lord, to receive glory and honor and power: for thou hast created all things, and for thy pleasure they are and were created" (Revelation 4: 11).

Jesus is the Word, the Way, the Truth, and the Life. (John 1:1, 14:6)

"The earth is the LORD's, and all its fullness, the world and those who dwell therein. For He has founded it upon the seas, and established it upon the waters" (Psalms 24:1-2).

God created the heavens and the earth and everything that exists, including humankind. Therefore, we all belong to God. No one exists by his or her own choice, or through any deliberate action of their own. Neither have we evolved from apelike ancestors. It is just a figment of modern thought to think that human beings came into existence by a quirk of fate, or by some accidental combination of circumstances.

On the other hand, it is also incorrect, to believe that human beings will turn into other creatures after death, based on some kind of "karma." Anyone who thinks that is spiritually deceived. God clearly tells us in His Word the origin of man.

The Word

Jesus (the Word) Himself resisted the devil and made the devil flee from him. In so doing, He confirmed the Scripture which says, *"Submit yourselves therefore to God. Resist the devil, and he will flee from you"* (James 4:7). The devil has no choice but to obey God's Word, and he will flee when you submit yourself to God and resist him. Move on, always praising God in hymns, prayer and supplication. Don't forget to "eat," meaning, remember to read the Bible, His Word. One little word spoken by Jesus defeated the enemy. So, it is important for you to know the Word of God and that you apply it to any circumstance.

If you study the Bible daily, you could read through the Bible three or four times a year. Most of the time, as I read my Bible, I listen to what the Holy Spirit is saying at that moment, and then I write that revelation on the blank space near the verses I am reading. I am amazed how He, the Holy Spirit, will reveal new things to me each time I read the same Scripture. That is why we should continually be in the Word, and consider it our manual for life. God is concerned about His Word. So, we should use the Word to praise Him; speak the Word into our circumstances; and, refer to the Word in our prayer.

Thank God regularly for His Word. Speak to people using His Word. When you greet people, say *Shalom*, which means "peace." When Jesus appeared to His disciples following His resurrection, He greeted them with, *"Peace be with you..."* Rest on the Word by waiting and listening to what God has to say to you. In Isaiah 55:11, God promises that His Word will not return to Him void (unfulfilled); but that it will accomplish whatever He sends it to do. God respects His word. He is concerned about you using the Word. God has made some direct pronouncements in the Holy Bible about His Word (the Bible). He expects us to take advantage of those pronouncements. He said, *"Come now, and let us reason together..."* (Isaiah 1:18a). He also says, *"Command ye me"* (Isaiah 45:11b). My friend, learn the Word; know the Word; and use the Word. God is concerned about you using His Word.

> [31] *What shall we then say to these things? If God be for us, who can be against us?* [32] *He that spared not his own Son, but delivered him up for us all, how shall he not with him also freely give us all things?* [33] *Who shall lay any thing to the charge of God's*

elect? It is God that justifieth. ³⁴ Who is he that condemneth? It is Christ that died, yea rather, that is risen again, who is even at the right hand of God, who also maketh intercession for us. ³⁵ Who shall separate us from the love of Christ? shall tribulation, or distress, or persecution, or famine, or nakedness, or peril, or sword? ³⁶ As it is written, For thy sake we are killed all the day long; we are accounted as sheep for the slaughter. ³⁷ Nay, in all these things we are more than conquerors through him that loved us. (Romans 8:31-37).

A Carrier of God's Glory

Is God concerned about you when you are being persecuted? He absolutely is! And the best news is that He can, and will, see you through. Do you remember the three Hebrew men who were thrown into the fiery furnace? They were Shadrach, Meshach, and Abednego. And, do you recall how suddenly a fourth person appeared in the furnace with them, and stood next to them amidst the flames?

King Nebuchadnezzar, who had them thrown into the fire, confessed, *"Lo, I see four men loose, walking in the midst of the fire, and they have no hurt; and the form of the fourth is like the Son of God"* (Daniel 3:25) Indeed it was Jesus who appeared in the fire to protect the three men. Just because you don't see Jesus physically with you does not mean you are alone. You are never alone. His holy angels are always at work assigned to minister to us all the time. (Hebrews 1:14)

The Holy Spirit (the Spirit of The Most High God) is always ready to comfort you. He resides in your heart. So, allow Him to take over every part of you (body, soul and spirit), and you will see the manifestation of God. You will experience His protection and life-changing power. *You* are His dwelling place, His sanctuary, a glory carrier. Yes, you! You are special, very unique, and different. You are not lucky, you are blessed and highly favored. The eternal Creator God of Heaven lives inside you!

So, why panic when He tells you to go into the world and spread the gospel. Just go! You aren't going alone, are you? Not at all. Jesus, "the fullness of the Godhead bodily" is in you. Like the three in the furnace, who became four; I count Father, Son, Holy Spirit, and you. That also makes four! I sometimes hear Christians say, "I am lonely." How can that be, when the blessed Trinity is forever with you — in you!

He is concerned about you not being alone. The Alpha and Omega (God) loves you. He knows your need and is ready to help you. Are you receiving the revelation? Ask Him lots of questions, and you will discover that He is there to answer.

For instance, when you misplace your keys, or you can't think straight because you are under a lot of stress or pressure, ask the Holy Spirit to show you where your keys are. Ask Him to give you a sound mind. Don't go about confessing negative thoughts, or speaking things that are contrary to His Word; and then turn around and say that you were only joking. You may hurt people with your unkind words when you do that. Remember, the Scripture encourages us in Ephesians 5:4 to avoid *"filthiness, nor foolish talking, nor jesting, which are not convenient: but rather giving of thanks."*

> *"For as he thinks in his heart, so is he..."*
> (Proverbs 23:7).

> "A good man out of the good treasure of his heart bringeth forth that which is good; and an evil man out of the evil treasure of his heart bringeth forth that which is evil: for of the abundance of the heart his mouth speaketh" (Luke 6:45).

> *"And they overcame him by the blood of the Lamb, and by the word of their testimony; and they loved not their lives unto death"* (Revelation 12:11).

Jesus is life, because He is alive. He arose from the dead. Founders of other religions have died. Their bodies have decayed, awaiting the second coming of Jesus, the King of Kings, who will raise up the dead and judge the world. Oh, and don't forget that we shall rule and reign because He has made us to be kings. How exciting! Get ready, because His Word and Promises are true.

Before I accepted Jesus as my Lord, I loved Him, and God the Holy Spirit. *How?* You may ask. Have you heard people say, when something occurs, "I knew that was going to happen?" How did they know? It's intuitive. Something within me made me feel that I would encounter Jesus someday. Have you felt that way? What is it?

He Cares

You have the spirit of God dwelling in you, you were created in His image, but it is just that you don't have a relationship with Him because you don't spend adequate time with God, your Father. That is, if you are a Christian and you don't hear God's voice, it means you are not being led by His Spirit. That means you are still self-willed, not God-dependent, but rather depending on yourself and your own power.

Imagine you are piloting an airplane, in the air, and without any training whatsoever. You are not prepared for trouble, and are bound to crash. I'd much prefer that the Lord pilot the plane, with the Holy Spirit as His co-pilot. I want Him to oversee the journey. Then, I can take a back seat and expect His travelling mercy.

I received that understanding after I survived a terrible automobile accident. I am alive, thanks to Jesus. After the accident, He gave me a revelation of me sitting in the back seat, leaving the driving to Him. How peaceful. Total surrender! That means I am not on my own. (1 Corinthians 6:19-20) Rather, Christ Jesus is Lord of my life. Therefore, I say, "Drive, Lord Jesus!'

Recently, I discovered that my maternal grandfather, who was in the Middle East during the Second World War, converted to Islam. I had always wondered why and how my family became Muslim. When he returned from the Middle East, he tried to convert everybody in his family to become Muslims. In 1999, the Lord asked me to write a book. I had no clue about writing, how or where to start, or, what the title would be. Again, He came in a vision and asked me to write, not just one book, but several books. He started giving me ideas about some titles. Sadly, I hesitated. I delayed. Since then, I have noticed that He appointed other people to write books with the same title that He gave me.

When I started writing this book, He gave me the title, and the color scheme for the cover. Hearing a few preachers address some of the topics in this book in their sermons; I knew that the Lord was reminding me again to go ahead and publish it. I tried to get help from others who have written books, but could not find anyone who would help me edit the book. A friend in England asked me to send her the manuscript, which I did. But, I never heard from her again. I thank God for them being honest with me, and I have absolutely no hard feelings at all.

When I started to write this book in 2004 my mother, who I love, was still a Muslim. I trusted the Lord that she would come into the Kingdom of God. However, she passed away on December 10th, 2005. I was so broken. I miss her dearly, and I cry anytime I think about her. The worst time for me is when I go to Uganda for a visit. The fact that she won't be there to greet me makes me so sad. It cuts me to the core of my heart. However, the Lord is continuing to heal and comfort me.

Someday I will write about what I call "holy mourning." Sometimes I cry when I think of how Jesus suffered for us, especially for me. When it occurs to me, I cry endless tears. You see, I was the first in my family to confess my sins and receive Jesus as my Lord and Savior. It was a decision I have never regretted. There is no turning back from Him. Jesus Christ is Lord. Jesus Christ is my Lord and my life forever. Amen!

Saved.... And All the Household!

The Lord has raised up people like me, who once practiced Islam, to uproot the root of Islam from our families and nations. As a result of prayer, Islam will crumble. *"Let God arise, let his enemies be scattered..."* (Numbers 10:35). For it is *"...not by might, nor by power, but by my spirit, saith the Lord of hosts"* (Zechariah 4:6).

On one occasion, when I went back to Uganda on a visit, I heard the sounds from the mosque early one morning. It bothered me. I inquired of the Lord about it, and He told me that Islam will crumble to the ground. In a vision, He showed me green grass on the ground. I am waiting for His words to come to pass.

I am not alone anymore. Many in my family have turned from Islam to the Lord Jesus. Some have yet to do so for fear of persecution. If they publicly confess Him, they would be disowned, or their parents would not pay their school fees. My dear friend, I assure you, that there is a war in the heavenlies. We, Christians, are tearing down principalities and powers, standing firm in Jesus' name, and seeing victory.

In Psalm 2:8 (NJKV), the Lord invites us, saying, *"Ask of Me, and I will give you the nations for Your inheritance, and the ends of the earth for Your possession."*

The Family

By the time I became a Christian, I had already lost a dear friend, my late brother, Safi Okabo. It's a pity because I don't think he knew Jesus. I also lost my sister Asher. By then I had become a Christian, but unfortunately I was not in Uganda to talk to her about Jesus, nor did I try to give her the message of the gospel over the phone. My hope is that, at the last minute, she asked the Lord to be her Savior.

From the telephone calls I received, I was told that her last words were; *"May God forgive me."* Then there was Zura, our youngest sister. I would write to her regularly, telling her about Jesus; and she would write back with questions and comments. After a series of these letters, she declared that she was persuaded that Jesus is Lord and accepted Him as her Lord and Savior. Since she lives in Uganda, and I live in Canada, the only way we could communicate was through letters, and the occasional phone call. However, I was still able to mentor her, and help her grow as a Christian. Eventually we began to speak to our other family members.

The critical one was my uncle, the late Smith Opon Acak, former Ugandan Chief Of Staff, who was in a maximum-security prison in Luzira. Since we had no physical way to reach Him, I prayed for him regularly, requesting that the Lord would make a way for him to be released and saved. The Lord promised me that he would indeed be released and saved. So, for ten years, I prayed for my uncle.

It is good the Lord gives us hope and insight into His Word, and the truth of His promises. He also gave me several revelations about my uncle. Some of those revelations about my uncle's condition were breathtaking.

God showed me how he was tortured in prison, which made me pray even more fervently for him. Some of his friends were freed, but he incarcerated longer than any of his friends. After numerous court cases, he won his freedom, and the military government had to pass a ruling to release him. To me, my prayers were answered, and the Lord had done as He had promised. God is faithful. What He says, He always does. I was excited to hear that my uncle was out of jail, but also sad. I feared that he might be re-arrested or killed soon after his release.

However, the greatest cry of my heart was to find out if He had surrendered his life to Jesus before he died. Sometime later, I received a letter from Uncle Smith, dated July 14th, 1998, briefing me about what had happened since we last saw each other eleven years ago in Lusaka, Zambia. He signed the letter, and then wrote PRAISE THE LORD! AMEN! In capital letters. I knew then that he was born again and bound for heaven. I was very encouraged by God's faithfulness. What He promised me, He had done. Uncle Smith was saved, and out of prison.

When God says something, our part is to believe and pray until we see the manifestation. Do not fold your hands and do nothing. It will only prolong your miracle, and you will end up calling God a liar. God is not a liar, He is Truth, and you will appreciate that more and more as you get to know more about Him.

Just as I had feared, Uncle Smith was killed not long after his release. When I heard the news that he had been killed, I said, "They killed his earthly body, but we will meet again at the trumpet sound."

You see, when I trusted Christ as my Savior, I wrote down the names of my loved ones and others I knew who were not saved. I began praying that the Lord would save them before they died. I didn't know much about how to pray, but I quickly learned that the Holy Spirit will teach us how to pray, and what to do. If we focus on Him and obey His Word, the answer will come in His time. Amen.

Loving the Unlovable

God is concerned about everyone in pain. He is especially concerned about their accepting Jesus as their Lord and Savior. Before Idi Amin, the first military president of Uganda died, I heard that he was sick and I felt bad for him. Before the coup, when he was a general in the army, he would visit in our home. As young children we would play on his lap. My, how he changed after he became the president. He became one of the most wicked leaders Africa has ever known. People do change, don't they?

However, regarding Amin, all I remember is that my parents had to leave their home and hide to avoid being arrested. Everything changed. We left our home and moved to the village with my uncle. My parents had to live separately, hiding in different places, in case one of them was discovered and killed, the other might still survive. The Lord asked me to pray for Amin. I didn't object. I just obeyed and prayed for him, and shortly after I started praying for him, he died.

God loves each of us, so let's not judge. He is the best judge. So, let's leave that to Him. God loved Amin, and not just him. He loves all those bad leaders, but He doesn't love the evil things they did, or are doing. God is concerned about them returning to Him. There is a chance for any person to call on God for help as long as they have breath. Whatever your situation is, you can still call on God for salvation, and be with Him in paradise. Remember, the two thieves who were crucified on either side of Jesus? One asked Jesus to remember him, and Jesus confirmed then and there that he would be with Him in paradise that very day. He was a repentant thief. Why wait to the last minute, though? Take note. *"For God so loved the world, that he gave his only begotten Son, that whosoever believeth in him should not perish, but have everlasting life"* (John 3:16).

My Elder Brother, Ali

Now that I have matured a bit in the Lord, the Holy Spirit gives me specific instruction about who, or what I should pray. He knows the mind of the Father. After all, the Holy Spirit is God Himself. Besides, my Uncle Smith, the next family member I had to pray intensely for was my elder brother Ali, our first-born. He had a liver problem. I told my little sister Zura, to buy some olive oil, to pray over it, and to anoint him in the name of Jesus. I asked her to bind the spirit of death, and ask the Lord not to take his spirit until he confesses that "Jesus is Lord." I always buy Bibles and wait for an opportunity to give or send them to people. That's the best gift I can give anyone who is not saved, or people who cannot afford one.

One day, the Holy Spirit said to me, "Be a Bible coordinator." So I bought a copy of Dr. Morris Cerullo's *God's Victorious Army Bible,* and asked Zura to take it to my brother, Ali. He accepted it, which was good. One day I received a fax from Zura telling me that Ali's health was deteriorating rapidly. So, I inquired of the Lord whether this sickness would end in death. God showed me a coffin being lowered into the grave. I faxed Zura back and told her to stay close to Ali until my mother returned home. I knew my mother would be an obstacle in our reaching out to Ali, especially since she had said that Zura and I had become Christians and were confused. I also urged Zura to ask Ali to give his life to the Lord Jesus. I told her specifically, "Be persistent and do not leave him, because Ali is going to die."

Zura listened, and stayed with him. Our mother grew tired and returned to her house. The minute our mother left, I was told that Ali asked one of his sons to call "Zura," and ask her to come to his bedside to read the Bible to Him. Zura rushed to his bedside and read a portion of the Bible to him, then she asked him to give his life to the Lord Jesus. Ali agreed and accepted Jesus as his Lord and Savior.

Shortly after that, he seemed to lose his ability to speak. Ali was rushed to the hospital for treatment that Sunday evening. The next day, he was still not speaking. On Monday, his sister-in-law, who knows the Lord, visited and greeted Ali with, "Praise the Lord." Ali, the new believer in Christ, replied, "Praise the Lord." Remember, he had not spoken since he was rushed to the hospital on Sunday evening.

Later, I was told that after he said "Praise the Lord," he started laughing, saying, "God is good." Then suddenly, he passed away, cheerfully. He went to be with the Lord. Glory!

I had just come from a prayer meeting, and was about to change and go to the mountain to pray and do the work of God, when I received this information. I glanced at the fax machine and saw that I had received several faxes telling me about "Ali's" departure to be with the Lord. I read the faxes, then lifted up my hands in worship instead of crying. I could not cry because my heart was at peace. I knew then and there that Ali was with the Lord. I knelt down to pray and thank God, and then just before I got up, the Lord said, "You have won the battle." I knew what He was talking about. It had been a battle, and it still is; but, the battle is the Lords! I dressed and left for the mountain to pray in peace, as if nothing had happened.

... And All Our Household

"Zura's" case was different. She told me she had AIDS, so we prayed for healing. Then one day, the Lord told me, "I want to take that girl home." I pleaded with God and said, "No, Lord, she has three children." The Lord gave us one and a half years of fellowship on the phone. Zura received the filling of the Holy Spirit; and, as soon as she was filled with the Holy Spirit, she quickly began to gain strength and be healed.

We would worship together on the phone and share the Word of God. The doctor didn't know why her health had suddenly improved. Then out of the blue, Zura informed me that the doctor wanted to put her on intravenous drips. I asked her why, since she could eat on her own. She confirmed that she had no problem eating. Then the next day, she informed me that the medical staff had excised a piece of her skin. This was really confusing, because I knew that they only did that to dead people. Only God knew what was going on in the hospital. For three days, I phoned the hospital and they would not let me talk to her. The nurse would tell me that she was no longer in the hospital. But I knew that she had no relatives to visit her, because she was alone in South Africa.

On New Year's Eve, December 31st, 2002, as I was preparing for the Morris Cerullo World Evangelism, *World Conference*, I went down on my knees to pray for Zura, because I had not been able to reach her by phone for the past three days. We had chatted almost every day prior to that. The Lord told me to pray for my sister, Fatuma. So, I started praying, and as I did, I suddenly felt "holy fire" over my back. (It was an intense heat.) At the time, I was on my knees, face down. I continued to pray, knowing that God was manifesting Himself with His holy fire. That is the way God sometimes manifests His presence. I love it. It is a feeling of deep, intense heat over your body. It is very real, very distinct, yet you know it is good, not evil, nor just your imagination. Some people say that this manifestation of the Holy Spirit is for cleansing, a deep cleansing of our spirits and souls. All I know is that, whatever He wants to do with me, I am willing for Him to do it. I will pray like King David prayed, "Take not your Holy Spirit from me." I pray for Him to do whatever He wants to do with me. Yes, I enjoy the holy fire of God. As I prayed, the Lord said to me, "It will bring you joy."

Then the phone rang. Usually I don't pick up the phone when I am praying, but my son was out of town at my brother's for Christmas and the New Year holiday. I sensed that my brother was calling, because we would take turns phoning Zura to demonstrate our love for her. I somehow knew something important had happened. I picked up the phone, and sure enough, it was my brother from Calgary. He told me that friends in South Africa had called, saying that Zura had gone to be with the Lord. I was not shocked or stunned, I just said, "Alright, I'm leaving for the United States in the morning. Let's make arrangements when I return from the *World Conference*."

I drove to the church to worship and fellowship like nothing had happened. The truth is, I was deeply comforted because I knew Zura had met the Lord and would be with Him forever. As scheduled, I attended the *World Conference*, and did not phone Uganda until I returned a few days later. When I called home, I spoke to my mother, expressing my sympathy and condolences. Mother said, "Rhema, your sister Fatuma is here." She then handed the phone to Fatuma.

"Praise the Lord," Fatuma greeted me.

Surprised by her greeting, I asked, "Why are you saying praise the Lord?"

"I am saved!" She said.

I jumped with joy and I felt goose bumps over my body. (Perhaps you just did too.)

Then Fatuma said, "Auntie So-and-so is here, she's saved; and grandma So-and-so is here, and she's saved…" She ran through a list of nine family members, nine of our relatives in one place, all of them born again! Unbelievable. That is the doing of only one person, the Lord Himself. Later, I found out that several other members of my extended family had also come to know the Lord. It was like "a tsunami of salvation" had gushed through my family, picking up people and dropping them into the Kingdom of God.

"Salvation" is no longer a strange word in my family, praise the Lord. Fatuma and I talked, praised the Lord and glorified His blessed name. The Lord confirmed what He had told me. Zura's death DID indeed bring joy.

"Precious in the sight of the Lord is the death of His saints" (Psalms 116:15).

I told the Lord, "Surely you have done great things." Salvation had popped all over my family like popcorn in hot oil. The devil cannot resist the holy fire of God. My family had to get saved. I love knowing that they've all come to the Lord. It is harvest time for me, and especially in the Kingdom. I remember that as I prayed at the conference in the U.S. the Lord said, "Put in the sickle." I swept the air as though I had a sickle in my hand, using it to gather grain. It was a prophetic act, even though I didn't know what I was harvesting at the time. All I knew was that the Holy Spirit was directing me. I simply obeyed. After all, the harvest is always good, and whether He says "yes" or "no," it is always for our good.

God is concerned about us trusting and obeying Him. He is concerned about everything, especially the salvation of our family members. He answers prayers. Go to the Lord, though your situation may not be exactly the same as mine. Call on Him. Trust Him, and He will bring it to pass. Whether it comes quickly or takes time, keep trusting.

Before all this, we lost a very protective brother in the year 2000 when the government soldiers raided our home at dawn one morning, and shot him eight times. Sadly, it does not appear that he knew the Lord. If you don't believe that Jesus is Lord, it only shows how ignorant you are of Him, His word and His Spirit. If you love yourself, you would want to know the truth and find answers to the issues of life. This is why you have to know Jesus—the Way, the Truth and the Life. *How do I know that?* You might ask. I know that because Jesus told me before I became a Christ-follower.

Jesus Reaches Out

Saint Mary's College is a private Catholic school for girls. My mother, God bless her, always wanted me to have the best of everything. She worked hard to send me to a Catholic boarding school, knowing it was very expensive. She also knew that I would be required to go to church if I was enrolled in that school. She put her religious reservations (as a Muslim) aside, and sent me to Saint Mary's College. That was a big sacrifice for a widow with eleven children. My dear mother was extremely hard-working, and made sure that we were well looked after. As I recall, we had much better food in our home than many of my friends who had both parents working to support their families. Occasionally, a husband would send his wife to my mother for training on how to run the home. That is how enterprising my mother was, and how much she was respected in the community.

Jesus first appeared to me at Saint Mary's College, wearing a white robe. He said; "Come, and I will take you to the Father." It happened twice. The second time he appeared to me, I obeyed and followed him, and he took me along. We climbed the seven steps to the seventh door. When I hear stories of Jesus appearing to certain Muslims in Egypt and other Islamic countries, I know it is true, because it happened to me. The Muslim calls Him "Isa," and many of them are coming to Jesus (Isa). It is usually because of their fear of family members that many Muslims are hindered from confessing Jesus openly. I encourage you to pray against the spirit of fear on their behalf. Jesus is alive and very loving. Many Muslims secretly love Jesus, because He is Lord, and we Christians love the Muslims, which is why we pray for them to be saved and come into a loving and living relationship with Him.

If you are a Muslim, you don't need to wait for Jesus (Isa) to appear to you before you believe in Him. In fact, the Bible says that those who believe, having not seen him, are blessed. After all, that is faith.

> *"7...that the genuineness of your faith, being much more precious than gold that perishes, though it is tested by fire, may be found to praise, honor, and glory at the revelation of Jesus Christ, 8 whom having not seen you love. Though now you do not see Him, yet believing, you rejoice with joy inexpressible and full of glory"* (1 Peter 2:7-8, NKJV).

You are going through all the religious motions to save your own soul. Please understand, Jesus died for us so our souls will be saved. Some mistakenly think that by believing in Jesus they are joining a religion. No, you are not joining a religion, you are being saved. Salvation isn't about a religion. It's about a relationship with God through His sinless Son, Jesus. Believe in Jesus before it is too late. Jesus is not about religion. He is the Truth, and the only Door through which we have access to God Almighty. Don't die without Jesus in your heart. It will be too late, and hell will welcome you into unquenchable fire.

> *"10 Of this salvation the prophets have inquired and searched carefully, who prophesied of the grace that would come to you, 11 searching what, or what manner of time, the Spirit of Christ who was in them was indicating when He testified beforehand the*

sufferings of Christ and the glories that would follow. 12 To them it was revealed that, not to themselves, but to us they were ministering the things which now have been reported to you through those who have preached the gospel to you by the Holy Spirit sent from heaven — things which angels desire to look into" (1 Peter 1:10-12, NKJV).

"Therefore gird up the loins of your mind, be sober, and rest your hope fully upon the grace that is to be brought to you at the revelation of Jesus Christ" (1 Peter 1:13, NKJV).

When you die without confessing Jesus as your Lord, it's too late. There are no second chances. (Hebrews 9:27) Don't wait until that last moment. You can say a prayer right where you are. You can ask for His forgiveness and ask Him to come into your heart. Then find a church and start fellowshipping with fellow believers. It really is a simple prayer, but you need to pray sincerely, believing that Jesus hears you as you pray. You can pray this prayer right now:

"Father in heaven, I am a sinner. Forgive me of my sins. Lord Jesus, come into my heart today, and be MY Lord. Fill me with your Holy Spirit, in Jesus' name, Amen."

Jesus has everything you are looking for—true eternal life. Sweet Jesus is my Lord. I love Him. No one can take Him from me, or from you, once you receive Him. He is our richest treasure. He is the lover of my soul, my true faithful friend, and I trust Him with all my heart.

I can tell Him anything and he loves me, and listens to me. You don't need anyone to come between you and Him. Speak to him yourself. He knows everything about you, and understands more about the human experience than anyone. Tell Jesus about your troubles, then bless him for all the good things he has done for you. Establish an attitude of gratitude. Be thankful.

I ask him questions like, "Jesus, what are we going to do today?" Because He and I are in it together. He has all the solutions and the answers to all of life's questions. In spiritual battles, He reassures me with, "We are winning." Or He'll tell me, "You have won the battle." Then I'll say, "Lord You fought, and won that battle." Sometimes He laughs. I love to see Him have fun with me. He is always there, and He rejoices with us. He loves and cares for you and me. *He is concerned.*

Pills That You Will Love

God is concerned about everything, especially about you. If you ask Him for wisdom, He will tell you what to do, or how to go about things. He might even ask you to be quiet, and not to say a word. He will give you the revelation of His word, which will quicken you, and life will have a different meaning. You will experience a beautiful, peaceful life, full of holy living and excellent meaning with the Three-in-One

Godhead dwelling in you. Jesus is Wisdom.

Who do you turn to for help? Turn to the Lord. He is concerned about you. You have fellow-believers to talk to as well. This is one of my daily readings. It is like a "gospel vitamin," which must be read regularly because it is so nourishing.

> *"17 that the God of our Lord Jesus Christ, the Father of glory, may give to you the spirit of wisdom and revelation in the knowledge of Him, 18 the eyes of your understanding[a] being enlightened; that you may know what is the hope of His calling, what are the riches of the glory of His inheritance in the saints, 19 and what is the exceeding greatness of His power toward us who believe, according to the working of His mighty power 20 which He worked in Christ when He raised Him from the dead and seated Him at His right hand in the heavenly places, 21 far above all principality and power and might and dominion, and every name that is named, not only in this age but also in that which is to come. 22 And He put all things under His feet, and gave Him to be head over all things to the church, 23 which is His body, the fullness of Him who fills all in all"*
> (Ephesians 1:17-23, NKJV).

Have you seen some Christians shining, radiant, looking more and more youthful every year, glowing from glory to glory? It is not their money. It is the gospel having an effect on them. I have experienced that in my own life. Here is one other "pill" I love.

> *"Who satisfies your mouth with good things, so that*
> *your youth is renewed like the eagle's"*
> (Psalms 103:5, NKJV).

You are what you eat. God is concerned about what you eat. The choice is yours— you can eat either junk food or fresh manna. His Word is fresh and very renewing.

> *"Behold, the fear of the Lord, that is wisdom, and to*
> *depart from evil is understanding"*
> (Job 28:28, NJKV).

God is concerned about every part of your life. He knows and understands everything about what is going on in our lives and what is best for us. Sometimes we think we know everything and can decide what we want, and how we should act. That's when we make the worst mistakes, and are forced to learn the hard way, because we did not ask Him. "Common sense" is a common term. Many people rely on their common sense. However, there is nothing like that in the Kingdom of God. It is best to ask the One who has all the answers. He says in His Word…

- *Ask of me…*

- *Whatever you ask in my name…* (the name of Jesus)

- *Ask and ye shall find…*

- *Call unto me, and I will…*

- *If we ask anything, according to His will...*

That is the shortcut I discovered from the Master. He is the Answer, the King of kings, and the Lord of lords. The fact is, we do not always know what is best for us, even if we feel we do. It's always best to go to our Father for confirmation before we act. It is not what we want that matters, but what He wants. We have desires and needs, and there is no doubt that He grants the desires of the righteous.

I was created for his pleasure. So, my prayer is that the desire of the Lord will be established in my life. Let us learn from His Word, the Bible. There are several examples of people wanting things they thought were good for them, who ended up regretting their decisions.

Look at the nation of Israel who asked for a human king to rule them; not knowing that God was their only true King. He gave them Saul.

In the wilderness, they could not wait for Moses to come back, so they created a golden calf to worship.

Today, many seek their own kind of messiah. But, God sent His only begotten Son, the only true Messiah!

Running After Other Gods

Another issue that has weighed heavily on my heart for a while is the state of many churches and Christians. It is common to find people who claim to be Holy Spirit filled men and women of God, who are committing fornication (sex before marriage), or adultery (sex outside of marriage). As a result, they often end up marrying the wrong person, getting divorced, and before they are healed from their previous sinful lifestyle, they start dating again. Incredibly, some in this condition even serve as ministers. The fact is, many have not repented, nor have they been healed.

The Word of God is clear. Each of us will be judged by the same book, the Bible. Everything we need is inside that treasured book. Now do not get me wrong, I am not condemning anyone, but the word "judgment" is in the Bible. The Prince of Peace makes it clear when in John 9:39a (NKJV), He says, *"For Judgement I have come into this world, that those who do not see may see, and those who see may be made blind."*

> *"17For the time has come for judgment to begin at the house of God; and if it begins with us first, what will be the end of those who do not obey the gospel of God? 18 Now If the righteous one is scarcely saved, Where will the ungodly and the sinner appear"*
> (1 Peter 4:17-18, NKJV)?

Remember also the story of the wise and foolish virgins. The good Lord told the foolish virgins, "depart from me, for I never knew you." There is time to return, therefore let us return to the Lord our Maker with all our heart, mind and soul.

Some Holy Spirit filled Christians are even marrying non-Christians, hoping they will get their new spouse saved. God warns us against that in 2 Corinthians 6:15. To me, that's like knowingly sleeping with the devil. He says that light can have no communion with darkness. I hear the Lord saying, "The church has gone the way of the world." Is the Holy Spirit wrong? There are even Christians going on the internet to get a wife or husband. Forgive them, Lord, because they can't wait, they are so desperate they do not know what they are doing.

Take a good look at many of our churches. When it comes to picking people for positions or for an office in the church, the emphasis is no longer about spending time in prayer or asking the elders of the church to pray for, and lay hands on the one the Holy Spirit chooses. It is rather about what the pastors think is good, or who has more money. Sometimes people are given positions in the church because their family is rich; because they have the right skin color, or share the same background as the pastor; or because they have the "right credentials" for that job or task. Discernment no longer plays a role. The question leaders need to ask themselves is, "Is this my church or it is the Lord's church." Remember, it is the Lord's. He died for it!

Every tribe, every tongue and nation will come and worship Him. Some pastors' wives are gossips. When young believers confide in them, very soon the details are all over the place. This sows discord, bringing strife instead of unity. In those situations, the prayer team intercessors are praying for unity, while the leaders are sowing discord and hurting the flock. It might not happen in your church, but it certainly does in many churches. This is why I say that it is better for you to confide in Jesus alone. He is a friend who sticks closer than a brother. Let's commit ourselves to pray and do things the Bible way. Remember, they are written as an example for us.

Therefore, when it comes to making important decisions, wait and be sure that you hear His voice. Why rush into bed with somebody you are not married to? You can pray, be friends, write letters, talk and *wait*. Once you are married, you are free to enjoy marital intimacy. In the process of waiting, if the Holy Spirit warns you against the relationship, then you have not become attached sexually, so there are no soul ties to break. In that case, you can bless each other and move on without guilt, and without becoming enemies.

Let's learn from our past mistakes, and from the mistakes that other people make. Fire is fire—it burns! The first time you put your hand into the flame you got burnt. So, why do it again? I am talking from experience. It is not just the young women who are involved, some older ones are involved too; behaving immaturely. I promise you, the Lord can take that desire away. Ask Him to take it away. He knows about sexual desire, so ask Him anything. Without Him we can do nothing; but, with him we can stand, do great things, and do exploits.

Is it because you are cold in the night? Why don't you tell Him–"it's cold, Lord." Ask him to warm you up. After all, He is a consuming fire. I have asked this not only at night, but even on some cold winter days as I stood outside. I have seen God's love and His hand, and I am in awe. One day I was tired and sore from work. There was no one to massage my aching shoulders and legs. I asked the Lord, "Father, would you send ministering holy angels to massage me?" He did, sending His angels, and when I awoke I felt their hands massaging my legs. (Hebrews 1:14)

This does not mean you stop praying for your marriage, or stop praying for your future soulmate. Some preachers even teach that obedience is not the key thing because God delights in us. While it is true that He delights in us, He does not delight in our disobedience and sin. His Son sacrificed His life to redeem us from sin and bondage. For God the Father to ignore our sin would dishonor His Son. I love the 28th Chapter of Deuteronomy. The Lord makes His Word clear that if you pray, He will warn you about the dangers ahead. You will then be left with the decision to obey Him or to be self-willed. He knows what is best, so we should learn to ask Him-who-knows-best. I thank Him because He only wants to give us what is best for our lives. His plans for our lives are only good, to bless us, and give us abundant life. I regularly bless Him and tell Him, *"Lord, I bless you; I bless you."* He is the One who died for me on that terrible cross. Yes, Jesus Christ, who lives in me, is the hope of glory. He was the One who was hanged, stretched, nailed, and crucified for us all. My heart is full of praise for Him. Now I must exalt His lovely name by singing this song.

Say the name of J-e-s-u-s;

Say the name of J-e-s-u-s;

Say the name most precious;

No other name that I know.

I will say His name J-e-s-u-s.

I fall in love with Him repeatedly, over and over. He is my all in all. I love my Lord Jesus. I trust Him fully, and know that I will not go wrong if I obey what He says. The same is true for you. He loves us dearly.

CHAPTER TWO

COMMUNICATION

*"But to do good and to communicate, forget not: for
with such sacrifices God is well pleased"*
(Hebrews 13:16).

God has spoken, and He still speaks today, even though
some say He only speaks to certain special people. Some
Christians believe that God no longer speaks, so they use
"common sense" or other intellectual means to make
decisions. They are not that different than other religions who
think God cannot speak directly to man, or has only spoken
once through a special prophet, or leader. Read through the
Old Testament and you will find many examples of God
initiating conversations with people like Abraham, Moses,
and Jacob. And God still speaks to Christians I know; such
people as Chuck Pierce of *Glory of Zion,* Dr. Morris Cerullo of
MCWE, Cindy Jacobs of *Generals International,* and to me. God
spoke to each of us before we were Christians. Now that I am
a Christian, I hear Him more, and hear more clearly. Jesus
said in John 10:27 "My sheep hear my voice." He is God, and
He can speak how and to whom He wants. If you haven't
heard His voice, ask Him to speak to you, He will.

I have not yet met any praying Christian to whom God
does not communicate intuitively (in their heart), or in
dreams, through visions, and through audible voice. God is

relational. He desires to communicate with us and will use every opportunity to reach out to us, because He is concerned about us knowing His truth.

Be At Peace with All Men

God is not like a man with an attitude problem who reacts angrily when treated badly. He does not hold or bear grudges. I used to be like that until I asked the Lord to help me deal with my attitude. I struggled with my attitude for years, with little success.

In 2005, I visited Uganda and stopped first at my elder sister's home. My plan was to go to my hometown later. However, news travels fast in Africa. My mother already knew I was in town, so by the time my sister and I left to go to our family house, my mother was already upset because I had not come to see her at the family home first. She was waiting for me and reacted with silence when I arrived. I knelt down to greet her, but she did not respond. Everybody just looked on, not making a comment. Then a four-year-old child standing near us said, "Your mother should get saved." We all laughed about it, but it was clear that my mother was upset because I had not come straight to the family house. Later on, I moved on to my sister-in-law's house where I usually stayed, since she was a Christian. We danced and praised the Lord, and then we had dinner. Eventually my mother sent a child with a message for me, and she finally came to greet me.

The following day, my mother's friends gathered together at our home. She only invited her Christian friends. I asked Kenny, one of my mother's close friends, about my mother's reaction to my visit. She explained that sometimes my mother would not speak to her circle of friends for days. I told Kenny that I had been behaving in the same way and had wondered from where I inherited that character flaw. Praise God for His deliverance. He has set me free from that behavior. Now when someone wrongs me, I am able to quickly forgive. If they try to ignore me, I will approach them and attempt to clear the air, or resolve the issue amicably. I do not want any anger, malice or bitterness to take root in my life. As an intercessor, it hinders your prayer life. I have no room for a display of that type of character. (Romans 12:18)

In His Presence

Why should you want God to talk to you if you do not call on Him? However, because He loves us and desires to help us, He might sometimes surprise us by starting the conversation Himself. I love Him for speaking to me when I least expect it. Or, when He speaks to me at times when my heart and mind are far away from Him. He reminds me of my mother during the times that I visit her in Uganda. She would come into my bedroom early in the morning, and even though I was still asleep, she would sit at my bedside talking to me. I believe she wants to catch up on the times that she has missed, due to my absence from the country. She's redeeming the time because she loves me.

The first time I went back to Uganda after being out of the country for years, she wanted to sleep in the same room with me. I said, "No, Aya. I am a grown woman now." It wasn't that I minded her sleeping in the same room with me; it was just that she would talk all night and deprive me of sleep. (Smile)

Growing up as a child, we were taught to greet the elders first. However, sometimes the Holy Spirit starts my day by greeting me "good morning" as I wake up. As His child, I am so happy because I love Him. I am excited to know that we have a Father who is so loving. Usually, I will reply, "Good morning, Daddy!" That greeting wakes me up, refreshes me, and I find myself very alert, not wanting the conversation to stop. It is just that I have to leave for work, and that hurts, because I do not want to leave His presence.

"How are you doing?" He will ask. He already knows how I'm doing, being God, but He wants to talk to me because He loves His children. In my case, He knows how I love to be reassured of His love, and presence. Every child is different. Some cannot be bothered, but I am always asking for more of Him. Since our needs differ, He knows and understands how to handle each situation. God is very friendly. He wants you to know He is with you, and that He cares when you are going through rough times. He shows up when you least expect him with an assuring presence. He reassures us of His love. Even when He comes like a fire, I am comforted, because He is God and can present Himself to us in any way.

God is concerned about you and how you sleep. He gives His beloved sleep, and He is concerned about how we wake up. He knows exactly when we should be awake to fellowship with Him, and at the same time, He gives us enough time to get ready to go to work. I have not used an alarm clock to wake me up for years. I got rid of that noisy machine, because

I would just pull the cover over my head and go back to sleep, and invariably end up oversleeping. Now the Great I AM wakes me up. Even when I am travelling and have to get up at an odd time to go to the airport, He will wake me up. Sometimes I tell Him to wake me up at such and such a time, and He does.

Once, my son and I were supposed to travel somewhere. I do not remember which mission trip it was, since we have been on so many. I did not want us to miss our breakfast on the flight that morning, so I asked the Lord to wake me up when they were serving the food. My son, Emmanuel, was very young and was sleeping at the time. When the air hostess was three seats away from us, I saw this huge tall, muscular person in my dream telling me to get up because they were serving the food. (I remember that I didn't see the face of the person speaking to me, just his form). I awoke, looked down the aisle and saw that the flight attendant pushing her cart, bringing food. That's how I grew to be so dependent on the Holy Spirit. I trust Him, because He is always accurate and on time. God is concerned about everything that concerns you. He cares for you more than you know.

"Now to Him who is able to do exceedingly abundantly above all that we ask or think, according to the power that works in us"
(Ephesians 3:20, NKJV).

The Reality of His Presence

"But who may abide the day of his coming? and who shall stand when he appeareth? for he is like a refiner's fire, and like fullers' soap" (Malachi 3:2)

"And the Holy Ghost descended in a bodily shape like a dove upon him, and a voice came from heaven, which said, Thou art my beloved Son; in thee I am well pleased" (Luke 3:22).

"And when the day of Pentecost was fully come, they were all with one accord in one place. ² And suddenly there came a sound from heaven as of a rushing mighty wind, and it filled all the house where they were sitting. ³ And there appeared unto them cloven tongues like as of fire, and it sat upon each of them. ⁴ And they were all filled with the Holy Ghost, and began to speak with other tongues, as the Spirit gave them utterance" (Acts 2:1-4).

The Holy Spirit is real, and He wants to manifest Himself to us. I have grown to become aware of His presence and manifestation, and I long to know Him more and more in the deepest way. So, I must seek Him more. When He chooses to touch me with His holy fire, it makes me love Him still more. Have you experienced His manifestation in your life? How about the times when you are fellowshipping with Him, and there are no windows open or any air conditioners on, and suddenly He breathes on you?

When I first started experiencing this, I used to open my eyes to see what was going on, because most of the time, I pray with my eyes closed so I can focus. That way, there are no distractions, so when He is revealing something to me, I can be certain about it. Now when a sudden wind starts blowing in the room, I now understand that He is there with me, walking on the "wings of the wind,"' and I continue to worship or pray, without fear or anxiety because I want Him to finish what He wants to do.

"Bless the Lord, O my soul. O Lord my God, thou art very great; thou art clothed with honour and majesty. 2 Who coverest thyself with light as with a garment: who stretchest out the heavens like a curtain: 3 Who layeth the beams of his chambers in the waters: who maketh the clouds his chariot: who walketh upon the wings of the wind"
(Psalm 104: 1-3).

God is with His people, and when He says *"I will never leave you nor forsake you,"* He means what He says. Even though He is not in the same form, as two thousand years ago, when He walked the dusty roads of Israel, He still does wonders and will do much more than when He was on Earth in the form of a man—God incarnate, Jesus Christ. My dear friend, strive for and desire a more intimate relationship with the Lord and you will encounter marvelous thing with Him. Imagine walking hand in hand on the holy mountain with him. You may encounter the glassy sea with Him, and view the seraphim and cherubim, even though you will not see His face, lest you die. There is still work to be done and battles to be won with Him on planet Earth.

The Work of the Lord

Talking about work to be done, one day I was at a conference hosted by Dr. Morris Cerullo. He was scheduled to travel to the Middle East after this conference, and being a humble servant of God, he asked us to cover him and his team in prayer during the time that he would be ministering to the Muslims. After the conference, I flew home. The next day, I went to the Pilgrim Book Store, and bought a new worship CD, and went home to listen to it and to worship. After some time, I fell asleep on my living room floor. That is when I received a profound vision. I saw Jesus on the mountain in the desert, and I found myself on that mountain. But somehow I was not in the desert.

Suddenly, I saw Jesus again, this time in a valley in the desert, but I was still on the mountain. As I looked down into the valley, I noticed that the enemy of our souls, the devil, was right behind Jesus. I yelled like a kid who loves her daddy, trying to warn Him so He wouldn't get hurt, "Lord, look behind you!" He didn't, instead He just moved one of his legs back and tripped the enemy, and then all I could see was the Lord marching forward. I started laughing. I was so happy because I knew then that the battle was won, Amen! Let's pray for each other, and especially for those of us on mission trips.

Let us not hesitate to evangelize. It doesn't matter which nation we are sent to, because the Lord is there to back us up. "Go to the nations and spread the gospel", I always hear Him saying. I answer with a, "Yes, Lord! Let me save some money for the airfare and I will be on my way." He has assured us of His presence anywhere we go.

The first time I heard Him sing to me was on a plane, on the way to a mission trip. I recall that I was reading a book by Max Lucado. Out of the blue, I heard the Lord's voice singing these words:

"Anywhere you go, I will go with you."

I sang back to Him

"Anywhere you go, Lord, I will go with you."

God is always there, whether or not there is a need. All we have to do is follow and He will do great things through us. He anointed Jesus of Nazareth, who went about doing good, rather than accumulating wealth, buying houses, and owning several cars that would be left here on earth.

I bought a new car in 2001, and I enjoyed it for a short time, but soon realized that this car was not satisfying all my needs. I felt something was wrong. I couldn't travel to do the assignments the Lord had asked me to do. I felt the financial strain of maintaining the new car, with car payments, increased insurance, and other costs. I realized then that I should have stayed with my old car, and sometimes I still dream about my old car. It was all paid for.

Then the Lord sent a visiting pastor to our church, someone who did not know me or what was going in my life. As he preached, he received a Word of knowledge and said, "There are some of you here, who can't go and do the work of the Lord because of a stupid car." My friend seated beside me looked at me because she knew who that "word" was for. I also knew that the Lord was reaching out to me. Shortly after, the car left my life. I was involved in an accident that left the car as a total write-off, however nothing happened to me—no injury, nothing.

That was the third car I had bought, believing that as a single mother, I would need a brand new car so that no mechanic could cheat me. To my mind, if I changed the oil and took care of the car, I would have at least five trouble-free years of use. But, I did not reckon with the costs of having a new car. I learned the hard way, since the car was a total loss.

- Did the Lord warn me against buying the car? Yes.
- Did He caution me to use the bus instead? Yes.
- Did I listen to Him, and use the bus? No.

When we devote all of our resources to things of this life, we are not able to support missionaries or the work of God.

Will we stand before the Lord empty-handed without having one soul, because of material things? Will we spend all our resources on material things, and watch others go to hell? Or, will we go?

Don't worry about language barriers if God has asked you to go somewhere. He will provide interpreters for you. Just go. It is fun to depend upon the Lord. Whether you are single or married, make plans to do the work of the Lord. Wherever you are, do the work of God in your local church. Get involved in one or more things. You can do all things through Christ who strengthens you. (Philippians 4:13) When the time comes to go—GO. God is concerned about people perishing. He is concerned about where you go.

The Holy Spirit is very real. As Bill Gaither's song says, "He touched me; Oh, He touched me..." How do you know if somebody has touched you?

One year, while I was attending Dr. Morris Cerullo's World Evangelism Conference in Denver, Colorado, he specifically asked for people of African descent to go up to the altar to pray for our nations. I was on the first row at the time, and as we prayed, I felt a hand on my forehead. Because I am sensitive to who lays hands on my head, I opened my eyes to see who it might be. Remarkably, there was nobody there. That was my first experience of really knowing the touch of the Lord. Then, He began giving me visions of Him walking among the people at the conference, laying hands on some of them, though not on all. I asked what He was imparting. He answered, "Elijah's anointing." Then I began to hear preachers at the conference address that same topic. He is anointing those He knows will use the anointing for the right purpose. His anointing is not given to someone who simply wants to feel goose bumps, experience laughter, or whatever phenomenon, yet stay in one place without doing His work.

Always check with the Lord when someone comes to you with a word of prophecy, a vision, or a new direction. Some have received "prophecies" that they should go to the mission field, and they acted on those "prophecies" without checking with the Lord, to see if it was indeed His will. In the process, marriages have collapsed; while those who gave the "prophecies" kept their marriages and homes. I learned this the hard way. Our Lord is sweet. He loves people who, like children, will ask Him questions, and trust His answers. When He says or shows me something I do not know or understand, I keep asking for clarification. I'll ask Him:

- What is that?
- What does that mean?
- What are we going to do now?
- How are we doing?
- I did not hear, could you repeat that please?

Like a child, I don't like to see Him, my Father, leave me. So, I will try to do all that I can to stay alert and awake when I pray so that He can spend more time with me. He is polite, and He is concerned about us being kind and polite to others as well. We are not to be so overcome by passion or emotion that we are impolite. He is passionate, but He is kind and polite to His people at the same time. The Bible is full of God's encounters with His people.

"Then He finished talking with him, and God went up from Abraham" (Genesis 17:22).

"So the LORD went His way as soon as He had finished speaking with Abraham; and Abraham returned to his place" (Genesis 18:33, NKJV).

In His Presence

This is not just in the Old Testament. How about Jesus' encounter with the early disciples after His resurrection? Since the day he touched me, our relationship has flourished. I enjoy Him, and I always say, "Lord, not only more of you; I want all of you, Lord." I want to linger longer in His presence. Even when the Lord has said what he wants me to hear during a time of prayer, I will still linger a little longer just in case He wants to say something else. I have an unquenchable desire to experience more of Him. After a time of prayer, I will typically go to the Word, and sure enough, He continues speaking to me from where we left off minutes ago. This is Divine Love.

One day, I was in my kitchen, aware that I would be based in Canada, and traveling to various countries on missions as He would instruct. As I reflected on this, I heard Him say,

"Lo, I Am with you always." I didn't say a word, but the Lord knew what I was thinking that very moment. He was reassuring me that He would be with me. That's true love. I know He loves me very much, I don't doubt his special love for me. I wish that everyone could feel and experience His love. Though many who doubt it, the fact remains, He truly loves them; and you! Why am I saying this? I'm saying this because I have fellowship with many Christian brothers and sisters who do not experience this kind of fellowship on a daily basis. Theirs' is more of an "on and off" relationship with Him. They have yet to experience that level of intimacy with God.

I remember meeting a sister who was older than me, and had been a Christian for several years longer. As we fellowshipped, she began to sing. I did not know the song, so I couldn't join her to sing it. She harshly judged me saying that I couldn't be a Christian if I did not know that song. She had a very condescending attitude. No wonder she couldn't hear the voice of God. The Lord Himself told Peter that when he was strengthened, he should encourage the brethren; not that he would look down upon them. Sometime later, she confessed to me that her relationship with the Lord was so broken that heaven felt like a sheet of brass, very much in line with the warning given in the book of Deuteronomy.

"And thy heaven that is over thy head shall be brass,
and the earth that is under thee shall be iron"
(Deuteronomy 28:23).

If we have been believers for a long time, but have neglected seeking His presence, we shouldn't expect to experience it. We should not be deceived into thinking that having been a Christian for decades guarantees His presence. We need to maintain constant fellowship with the Holy Spirit, in the Word, in worship, and in prayer. We need to constantly examine ourselves and be sure that we are in right standing with Him. If we fail to constantly fellowship with Him, He will focus His attention on someone who does value His presence. The fact is, we need to learn and understand more about the character of the God we serve.

> *"Now all these things happened to them as examples, and they were written for our admonition, upon whom the ends of the ages have come. Therefore let him who thinks he stands take heed, lest he fall"*
> (1 Corinthians 10:11-12, NKJV).

The Lord always responds to the person who loves Him. Express your love for Him regularly, and listen to what He will tell you in response. He does not hesitate to shower His love on you when you express your love for Him.

> *"And when they had sung a hymn, they went out to the Mount of Olives"*
> (Matthew 26:30; Mark 14:26, NKJV).

"Let the word of Christ dwell in you richly in all wisdom, teaching and admonishing one another in psalms and hymns and spiritual songs, singing with grace in your hearts to the Lord"
(Colossians 3:16, NKJV).

When you sing to Him, adoring Him, He will show up. The Bible says in Psalm 22:3, *"But You are holy, Enthroned in the praises of Israel."* Which pastor or elder of a church just sits, or stands there, watching people worship, and then starts preaching? Not in my church, certainly not to my Jesus. Where did we get that knowledge from? Jesus came in the flesh two thousand years ago to show us the way to live a Christian life. Read His book to learn more from Him. As the children's song says,

The B. I. B. L. E.,

Yes that's the book for me;

I stand alone on the Word of God,

The B. I. B. L. E. Bible!

The Bible, God's book, tells us all about Him. We learn that He came in the flesh, so He feels and hurts just like we do. How do I know that? In a family, for example, some kids are a nightmare for their parents, and some are like sunshine. So it is with Christians.

One day before I got out of bed, I heard the Lord speaking. However His voice was rather faint, and I realized that there was no doubt to me that the Lord was hurting and weary over one of His daughters. He wants to be loved too. Your mom and dad love you, don't they? But they also want to be loved, and are not just there to give you gifts, they want you to love them in turn. So, I asked the Lord, "What is wrong, daddy?" And he replied that someone had made Him weary. I was shocked. God Almighty gets weary? I didn't know what to do. The Lord reminded me of something from His Word, and suddenly it became clear to me. He made me read the first five words in Malachi 2:17, NJKV, which says, *"You have wearied the Lord with your words."* Ephesians 4:30 warns us not to grieve Him. Yes, we can weary the Lord and hurt His feelings.

I called one sister and found out what was going on. She despised and criticized the call of God on my life. Some people limit you because you are single, but God does not. After speaking with her, I was convinced that I had to go and lay hands on her to pray with her over the issues. Then the Lord reminded me of the message He had given me concerning her. I had to obey. So after ministering to her, I told her what the Lord had revealed to me. She was shocked, and said, "You didn't tell me before."

I replied, "1 thought you wouldn't receive it, coming from me."

That night, on our way to see her, I grumbled that these people despise me because I am not married, so I didn't want to go and pray for her. I had to repent of that grumbling and then went to minister to her. The Lord intervened in her life and saved her. She had a heart attack and survived it, and is still alive today. God created us in His image, so He loves us, even though we weary Him sometimes, as the quote from Malachi says. So, love Jesus. Don't weary Him, grieve Him, or grumble. A servant does what the Master tells him to do.

God is concerned about all His children. His rain falls on the just and the unjust. So, who are we to judge? God is concerned about your heart, and He wants to heal you completely. He is able to heal you from any disease.

"For the Lord God is a sun and shield; the Lord will give grace and glory: no good things will He withhold from them that walk uprightly. O Lord of hosts, blessed is the man that trusteth in thee" (Psalms 84:11-12).

I Will Wait On the Lord

He loves to talk, especially to his children. Sometimes we are so impatient, we want to say all we have to say and leave. When I do that, He corrects me, telling me to linger longer and give Him time to talk to me. True, it's hard in our day and age to wait.

One day, I was so preoccupied with what I wanted Him to do, (even though He had already given me a set time), but there I was fretting. Because He knows our thoughts, He told me to relax. All I could say was, *"Lord, I am sorry."* God truly cares for all our needs. A couple of times, I have heard the

Holy Spirit telling me, verbally, that all my needs are met. (2 Peter 1:3) To Him, it is done, but as human beings, we can't wait to see the manifestation of what He says is done. But the fact is that, when He says it is done, *it is done*. Our task is to walk in the finished work, in worship, prayer, fasting, warfare, thankfulness, repentance, forgiveness, restitution; and the list goes on, according to what He reveals to us.

God will speak and reassure us wherever we are. I remember the first time He spoke to me at work. I was busy sorting mail during the night shift, quite sleepy at the time, then suddenly I heard Him say, *"All of your needs are met."* Mail went flying out of my hands since I had never had that experience at the workplace. I was startled. It was so unexpected. I suppose thought I had left Him in my bedroom where I usually spend time with Him in prayer, but now it was clear to me that He wanted me to know He goes everywhere with me. I remembered the song that He sang to me on that flight: "Anywhere you go, I will go with you." Perhaps I had limited God in my mind, thinking that the song referred to some far away mission field. But now, on reflection, where is the mission field? The mission field is actually wherever we are. He is in us, so everywhere we go, He is also there. Remember, we are the temple of the Holy Ghost. If you receive and accept this revelation in the depths of your heart, you will never again say you are weak *"because greater is he that is in you, than he that is in the world"* (1 John 4:4b).

That experience of hearing Him speak to me at work was the beginning of His constant reassurance to me about His presence. It was as if He was saying, *"I know where you work, and I'm there with you as well."* Honestly, God gave me the job through a revelation, saying to me, *"Canada Post is hiring."* His favor in my employment and workplace has been critical, because if it wasn't for His presence at my workplace, I could have been very frustrated looking for employment that would allow me to serve Him the way He wants me to.

I thank God for being omnipresent, and for being my number one Boss. He is everywhere and sees all things. So, whatever you do, save yourself the heartache and do everything unto the Lord. Jesus is the number one Boss, the friendliest, most wonderful Boss anyone could have. He cares for his employees [servants/His children] and is a Good Shepherd to his sheep. He communicates with me a lot at my workplace—showing me what to do, where to go and pray—all sorts of things. I know He is with me all the time. He comes and tells me so.

I give all the glory to God Almighty, because He is the source of life. I am His little girl; and you are His little child. He watches over all of us. I trust Him and can share everything with Him, knowing He will not betray my trust. On more than one occasion, when it was time for me to leave home to go to work, I found that I was reluctant to leave His presence, so I lingered a bit longer. Then I had to rush to work knowing I was going to be late. As I rushed out, He called my name, "Rhema!" When I turned around to see who called me, I saw no one. So, I responded, "Yes, Lord." Then I continued jogging to catch my train, so I could get to work on time. When I got to work, I went to punch my time-card, but there were no cards to be found. The supervisors had removed the time-cards, so I didn't have to punch in late. The Lord had even taken care of the time-cards! That was His way of protecting me and rewarding me for spending time with Him. If you spend time talking to your boss, and you forget to do something that you were required to do during that time, would he or she punish you? No!

Lord you are my help, *"The Lord is my shepherd I shall not want"* (Psalm 23:1).

We need Him all the time; and we need His fullness to be imparted into us.

"I am my beloved's, and my beloved is mine: He feeds among the lilies" (Song of Solomon 6:3, NKJV).

Who is the lily of the valley? Jesus.

"I am the rose of Sharon, and the lily of the valleys" (Song of Solomon 2:1).

If you don't talk to God your Father, how are you going to know what is going on in your life, or in the camp of your enemy? The Holy Spirit is our "heavenly Spy," and as we communicate with the Father on a daily basis, we will learn and know more; all to our benefit.

God is concerned about everything, especially about communicating with you.

CHAPTER THREE
INNER BEAUTY RADIATES OUTSIDE

Look at your head, see where He placed it. He designed the hair to grow and cover only a part of your head, leaving your neckline and your face to show just the way He wants it to look—beautiful.

> *"I will praise thee; for I am fearfully and wonderfully made: marvelous are thy works; and that my soul knoweth right well"* (Psalms 139:14).

He molds us perfectly. Even if we love ourselves so much that we try surgery and other things to enhance our looks, we cannot meet His standard for our faces. He is the Master Designer.

> *"But now, O Lord, thou art our father; we are the clay, and thou our potter; and we all are the work of thy hand"* (Isaiah 64:8).

Spiritually, He continues to mold us until we become the spiritually mature people He created us to be. He wants to restore us to His original plan—that we will bear His image.

He gives beauty for ashes. I want to be beautiful from the inside out, so I asked the Lord, and He has done wonders. When you hear a compliment about how beautiful you are, of course you say, "Thank you." We should pray, "Lord, make me beautiful like you. Make me beautiful from the inside out, and let the inner beauty radiate on the outside, shinning, giving you all the glory."

The Lord has done mighty things in my life. You need not go for a facelift as long as you stay in His presence. He will even provide extra things you did not ask Him for, because what He does is perfect for you. He is the Great Beautician. Yes, Jesus is. He will give you beauty for ashes. You will glow. You might even try to put a bit of powder or make-up on your face to cover the glow, but it will still penetrate, and you will shine. You cannot hide His handiwork, especially when He wants to show off with what He has done in you. Even your enemies will admit and confess that you look great, and will want to know your secret. When that happens, allow that to become a doorway for you to introduce Jesus into the conversation. When that happens to me, I declare that God renews my youth like the eagle, and satisfies my mouth with good things. As the Scripture says;

"But those who wait on the LORD Shall renew their strength; They shall mount up with wings like eagles, They shall run and not be weary, They shall walk and not faint" (Isaiah 40:31, NJKV).

Reading His Word is like taking vitamins for your spirit, soul, and body. Spend time with Jesus, and He can tell you what to wear, what to eat, what colors looks great on you, and other details that you might never have considered. However, the purpose of His doing that is to give you a chance to introduce Him into the conversation. Just the mention of His name is wonderful. Many have asked me if I am a model. I always reply, "Yes, for Jesus." They laugh when they hear that, but to me that is joy. As far as I am concerned, His name has been lifted up in the situation. I know that He will finish the work in His own way, because someone has to plant the seed, then another person will water it, and God will give the increase. Amen! (1 Corinthians 3:7)

"Arise, shine; For your light has come! And the glory of the Lord is risen upon you" (Isaiah 60:1, NKJV).

Moses tried to cover his forehead after he had spent time in God's presence, but He could not cover God's glory. Do you want to look stunningly beautiful, live long, and die with strength and good eyesight? The way to do it is to stay in His presence, worship Him continually, and to remember to take your vitamins—His Word. That is vital!

"And Moses was a hundred and twenty years old when he died: his eye was not dim, nor his natural force abated" (Deuteronomy 34:7).

"Honor and majesty are before Him; Strength and beauty are in his sanctuary" (Psalms 96:6, NKJV).

He changes us from glory to glory, Amen.

"The spirit of the Lord God is upon me; because the Lord hath anointed me to preach good tidings unto the meek; He hath sent me to bind up the brokenhearted, to proclaim liberty to the captives, and the opening of the prison to them that are bound; To proclaim the acceptable year of the LORD, and the day of vengeance of our God: to comfort all that mourn; To appoint unto them that mourn in Zion, to give unto them beauty for ashes, oil of joy for mourning, the garment of praise for the spirit of heaviness; that they might be called trees of righteousness, the planting of the Lord, that He might be glorified" (Isaiah 61:1-3).

God is concerned about everything, especially about our beauty, and how we look. We represent Him. We are Christ's ambassadors. (2 Corinthians 5:20) God loves us so much that He created us in His own image, and gave us His spirit, adding the oil of joy to keep us joyful. He is concerned about our beauty and happiness. Do you know that He also has a sense of humor? Have you ever heard the Holy Spirit laugh? Sometimes I have asked Him, "Lord, what are you laughing at? What is so funny?" God is fun to be with. He is happy, and full of joy.

When He is pleased with us, He shows gratitude, even saying, "Thank you." It is not because we have given Him something He cannot have; rather it is His way of declaring His pleasure. I want to know what gives Him pleasure so I can do it better and more often. Perhaps it is my personality, and how I was brought up, but I always want to be grateful and appreciative of the kindness He has shown to me. In one sense, God is a gentleman of the highest order.

"He that sitteth in the heavens shall laugh: the Lord shall have them in derision" (Psalms 2:4).

"The Lord shall laugh at him: for He seeth that his day is coming" (Psalms 37:13).

Perhaps you've seen people laughing uncontrollably in a worship service, and have wondered what was going on. That can be a sign that the Lord is reaching down with His healing, and anointing; laughing at the devil; and having fun with His children. He dresses us in the garment of praise, taking away our spirit of heaviness. (Isaiah 61:3) Then He compliments us. Awesome! Even though He did all the work, He still thanks, and compliments us. We have a lot to learn. God makes us righteous through His Son Jesus Christ, having sent Him to die for us on the cross. The cross was made of wood, and wood comes from a tree. Jesus is the Tree of Life, making us trees of righteousness. We, who are seeds of His righteousness, are to be fruitful for Him.

"And He showed me a pure river of water of life, clear as crystal, proceeding out of the throne of God and of the Lamb. In the midst of the street of it, and on either side of the river, was there the tree of life, which bore twelve manners of fruits, and yielded her fruit every month: and the leaves of the tree were for the healing of the nations" (Revelation 22:1-2).

"I am the vine, you are the branches: he that abideth in me and I in him, the same bringeth forth much fruit: for without me ye can do nothing" (John 15:5).

God is concerned about everything, especially about our healing and fruitfulness.

He loves to see us healthy, saying, "I Am the Lord, your healer."

"And he said, if thou wilt diligently hearken to the voice of the Lord thy God, and wilt do that which is right in his sight, and wilt give ear to his commandments, and keep all his statues, I will put none of these disease upon thee, which I have brought upon the Egyptians: for I am the Lord that healeth thee" (Exodus 15:26).

"He sent his word and healed them and delivered them from their destructions" (Psalms 107:20).

How can we pay Him or show Him our gratitude? There is no other way, but to admire, adore, love and worship Him. Fall asleep at His feet because there is no better place than in His presence. Can you imagine what eternity would be like? To be continually in His loving presence with perfect joy, peace, and contentment.

I recall being one of a group of intercessors who agreed to pray for a sister who had gone to be with the Lord. We were praying that she would come back to life, because we missed her terribly. We met twice to pray for the sister, but during the course of our praying, we received a revelation about her being asked to make a choice about whether to stay in glory with the Lord, or to come back to earth. Given the choice, she refused to return to earth. Who in their right mind would want to come back to earth after they've been called home to be with the Lord?

That is one lesson I have learned. Since then, I am reluctant to try to pray someone back to life. I have been tempted several times to pray that prayer for my mother, especially when I go to her grave in Uganda. I desperately want to shout, "In the name of Jesus, come forth." When a believer dies in the Lord, God takes the person into the spirit realm and they do not want to come back to earth. They are finally at rest, at peace in the presence of the Father. I sometimes long to go home to be with Him. When I am in His presence, I do not get hungry. I don't even think about food, because He is my Daily Bread.

Fasting As a Lifestyle

Fasting can become your lifestyle. It is a gift for all friends of the bridegroom, so if you cannot fast, ask for His grace to sustain you. There was a time when I thought that fasting a lot was weird. I would have the desire to fast, because I felt spiritually led by the Holy Spirit, who would say, "Fast, fast, fast."

I would reply, *"Lord, I am fasting."* I attended a meeting in Colorado Springs, the World Harvest Conference with Dr. Peter Wagner and the team. One of the speakers, Mike Bickle, spoke on the lifestyle of fasting, talking about the Mary's and Anna's of this generation. That was when I discovered that I was neither crazy, nor alone.

God is Concerned about Everything, Especially about Your Thoughts

God reveals things that will happen in the future, things to come. He reveals His secrets to His servants. Sometimes the Holy Spirit will tell me to go to a particular meeting, and when I get there, the speakers would unveil the Word and confirm what the Lord has told me. This is why God has ordained teachers, pastors, evangelists, prophets and apostles. Go to conferences and attend church services. Sometimes, near the end of a meeting, I have asked, *"What am I doing here?"* Then, before the meeting ends, I realize why I was sent there. There have been occasions when I did not feel up to traveling. I would wait until the last minute, and then rush to get myself ready for the trip, so I could attend a meeting as directed by the Holy Spirit. I am never disappointed when I arrive, because I always find some delicious "wild meat" out there.

We, the body of Christ, need each other. Unity is the call. I'm not saying that you should just go anywhere, to any conference, or to every church, because there are many out there, and not everyone who claims the name of Jesus is actually His disciple. However, allow the Holy Spirit to lead you, be prayerful and discerning.

One day I was fasting, and I felt so weak and hungry, I decided to break my fast. I wondered why I felt that way. The Holy Spirit told me to continue to pray, so I went to my bedroom, and there I entered His presence with praise and thanksgiving. After worshipping and praying, I got up and suddenly had so much strength, I felt I could run for miles. I continued to fast and pray.

Eventually, when the time came for me to break the fast, I forgot to break it until six hours later. Fasting does not kill you, as some people think. Instead, it does many interesting things, as we humble ourselves to the Lord. Our motivation is not to twist His arm to get what we want, but to realize that there is benefit and a reward in fasting. It is a shortcut to many answers to prayer, and makes us more receptive to revelations and ideas from the Holy Spirit, so don't hesitate to make fasting part of your life. Study the book of Daniel, especially Chapter Ten.

To me, fasting is a catalyst that exposes strongholds, and sharpens our discernment. It makes the "word of knowledge" come alive. In times of fasting, I am more alert, totally focused on seeking the face of the Lord for answers, especially in situations where prayer alone has not yet produced the results I was looking for.

Consider what the Lord told his disciples in Matthew 17:21, when they could not cast the demons out. He said, *"However, this kind does not go out except by prayer and fasting..."* Remember, even though Jesus had all of the answers, and knew all of the secrets, He still fasted. What about Apostle Paul? Do not hesitate to fast, it will not kill you, rather it will bring you lots of blessings.

There was a sister in the Lord, who had a whole pile of problems, and in addition to that, she was very lonely. Her children wouldn't visit or call her, even though they lived in the same city (Vancouver, Canada); and her sisters in England wouldn't communicate with her. Many times she would call me at work, very distraught, and crying on the phone.

After work, I would pick up my son from school, head home for dinner, and then later in the evening we would visit her to spend some time with her. After a few of these visits, I asked her to fast, and she replied that she would die if she fasted. People think that, out of ignorance. So, I explained to her what fasting involved. I managed to convince her to join me in a short fast, not a full day fast. During our time of fasting, the Lord revealed something really astonishing. I saw a demon tormenting her, then running to hell, or a hiding place surrounded by fire, knowing no one would follow it there.

In my vision, I dared to follow it to its hideout where it threatened me saying, "Don't come in here, you will burn." I didn't listen to that old lie, and I didn't reply. Rather, I went into the fire and pulled the lady out. I was not burned. In the vision, I also saw a third person there with us, a man who reminded me of the three Hebrew young men who were not burnt by the fiery furnace.

Shortly after our time of fasting and prayer, the lady's son called and asked if he could visit her. Then her sister in Manchester, England surprised her by sending her a ticket so she could visit them for Christmas. To cap it off, she had always been financially hard-pressed, always struggling to make a living, but now she is free from that also, and is financially much more secure. Eventually, her sister persuaded her to join them in Manchester. The family is united again. There is no doubt at all that prayer and fasting is another powerful weapon of spiritual warfare.

God is Concerned about Our Deliverance.

"2 In those days I, Daniel, was mourning three full weeks. 3 I ate no pleasant food, no meat or wine came into my mouth, nor did I anoint myself at all, till three whole weeks were fulfilled... 11 And he said to me, "O Daniel, man greatly beloved, understand the words that I speak to you, and stand upright, for I have now been sent to you." While he was speaking this word to me, I stood trembling. 12 Then he said to me, "Do not fear, Daniel, for from the first day that

you set your heart to understand, and to humble yourself before your God, your words were heard; and I have come because of your words. ¹³ But the prince of the kingdom of Persia withstood me twenty-one days; and behold, Michael, one of the chief princes, came to help me, for I had been left alone there with the kings of Persia. ¹⁴ Now I have come to make you understand what will happen to your people in the latter days, for the vision refers to many days yet to come" (Daniel 10:2-3; 11-14).

There is great benefit in fasting, and even if it should seem like you are not achieving anything, continue to fast. God's ways and His timing do not always make sense to us. But, He is God and has everything under His control. You may be tempted to eat and break your fast before the time you have set for yourself, but I encourage you to persevere. The fact is, fasting itself is so healthy that even non-Christians fast. They recognize its benefits.

For a Christian, fasting increases one's ability to exercise spiritual authority, and thus to be more effective in spiritual warfare. Why do you think some Christians are more effective in deliverance ministry than others? It is because you are what you eat. We are all called to do what Jesus did, and much more. Jesus fasted and so should we. He is our example and the greatest teacher of all time. The apostle Paul followed Jesus example. Read more about his life and ministry and how effective he was. The choice is yours. Luke 4:18 is part of my e-mail address, and I live it.

"¹⁸ The Spirit of the Lord is upon Me, Because He has anointed Me To preach the gospel to the poor; He has sent Me to heal the brokenhearted, To proclaim liberty to the captives And recovery of sight to the blind, To set at liberty those who are oppressed; ¹⁹ To proclaim the acceptable year of the Lord"
(Luke 4:18-19, NKJV).

I recall my involvement with a sister in the Lord who had a very sick child. The mother was in and out of hospital day after day. It was bad. I was furious with what the child and the parents were going through. I hate sickness and I asked the Lord, "What is this? This child is suffering, and the parents are tired." In my heart, I was ready for war, and I said to myself, *"I'm going on an Esther fast, nothing to eat or drink for three days, until the Lord reveals what is going on with this child."*

When I left their house going to the parking lot, the Holy Spirit told me what was wrong with their child. You may say it was not the fasting, but the Lord sees our hearts. Remember the story of Daniel. From the day Daniel set his heart to stand in the gap and inquire of the Lord, his prayers were heard. However, Daniel continued the fast for three weeks, although in the natural, nothing seemed to have changed.

In the spirit realm it was a different story. The angels had been assigned to deliver a message to Daniel from the first day that he set his heart to fast, but strongholds were trying to hinder the message from reaching Daniel. But we serve a mighty God and He has powerful representatives. When the Archangel Michael showed up on the scene, no demon in hell could stand, and Daniel received the answer to his prayer.

One night, I wanted to take a nap before I spent time in prayer. Big mistake! I should have stayed awake and prayed. This was a classic case of "sleeping on the watch." Does that sounds familiar? As I slept, I sensed that I was in a trench surrounded by demons. Even though they could not get to me, so I yelled, "Lord, send Archangel Michael." Like *Star Trek*, but faster; in an instant the Archangel Michael landed and the demons fled. That night, my prayer assignment was to pray for Vancouver, asking that God's glory would cover the city.

Back to the afflicted child, I still went ahead and called Sister Togo Kuhen and invited her to join me in a three day fast. After three days we went back to see the couple and tell them what the Holy Spirit had revealed. The truth is, we need God's grace every day to love one another, and to do things the way the Lord commissions us. When we intercede for someone, they don't have to be our next of kin or a close friend before we are prepared to sacrifice and go without food for them. The blood of Jesus binds us together irrespective of whether or not they are our close friends. Not only that, we are encouraged to fast and pray for non-believers also, because God is concerned about them. Remember, Jesus died on the cross for you long before you confessed Him as Lord and Savior. Let us not hesitate to be kind and caring, especially when we know what to do; or whenever it is in our power to help someone.

Loving by Grace

Without God's grace, we cannot love the way He wants us to love, and see as He sees. Couples, especially, need prayers. We need to ask the Lord to bless and sustain our marriages. Single believers also need prayer for the Lord to give them helpmates, and to help them refrain from fornication.

God is love. I love the way He loves us. We need to learn from the Master of Love, and ask for His grace to love each other as He loves us. I hear the Lord saying to you, "Let me look for a helpmate for you." In other words, don't search for one yourself, because you will mess things up. God is the Champion Matchmaker. I generally discourage people from looking for a helpmate on the Internet. (I am not saying that is what God has said, that is my personal view.) Instead of going to the Internet, go to God in prayer. You will be amazed what will be revealed to you in His presence. God wants us to love and to marry. Didn't He say in Genesis that it was not good that man should be alone? Has He changed?

In the year 2003 I heard the Lord say that it is good to obey, and to wait upon the Lord. If husbands and wives will submit to one another and love each other, things will get better; the church will get better; governments will be better; nations will come together and worship the King of kings, and the Earth will be filled with His glory. Sometimes even little things can be hard to do if we don't humble ourselves, and ask for Him to sustain us with His grace.

Once, when I was in England on an assignment, the Lord said to me, "Fight for grace." I was perplexed, thinking,

"What!? How can I fight for grace?" It wasn't long after I heard those words that He allowed a situation to develop that showed me what He meant, and something good come out of that assignment. Let's yield to the His Holy Spirit, listen to Him, and He will bless us. Let's worship Him!

You are holy, holy, holy, Lord God Almighty. You are righteous. Who is like you Lord? You are faithful, true and just, Mighty One. I love you, and may all the earth be filled with your glory. God of Abraham, Holy, holy, holy, Lord God Almighty, I adore you; I reverence you.

Most holy God, Jehovah, my Prince of Peace, I treasure you. My Source, my Strength, my Inheritance, my Portion, my Victor, My Source, you fight all battles for me, and make me a winner. Your love is amazing. You care so much for me. My great I AM!

God has a lot to do, yet He cares for, and has time for each of us individually. When we call on Him, He is always there for us and answers our prayers. He is our Guide, our Chief Director, and the Perfect Matchmaker. He knows our future. He wants us to pray for our marriages—are you praying for yours? Pray! God answers prayers, not tears. He answers prayers.

"And it shall come to pass, that before they call, I will answer; and while they are yet speaking, I will hear" (Isaiah 65:24).

It is time we started worshipping Him as the angels do in heaven. After all, we are seated with Christ Jesus in heavenly places. (Ephesians 2:6)

"8 And the four beasts had each of them six wings about him; and they were full of eyes within: and they rest not day and night, saying, Holy, holy, holy, LORD God Almighty, which was, and is, and is to come. 9 And when those beasts give glory and honour and thanks to him that sat on the throne, who liveth for ever and ever, 10 The four and twenty elders fall down before him that sat on the throne, and worship him that liveth for ever and ever, and cast their crowns before the throne, saying, 11 Thou art worthy, O Lord, to receive glory and honour and power: for thou hast created all things, and for thy pleasure they are and were created" (Revelation 4:8-11).

"Beauty is in his sanctuary. Honor and majesty are before Him: strength and beauty are in his sanctuary" (Psalms 96:6, NKJV).

Dancing to the Lord

How are you dancing, and where do you dance? One day, I was worshiping in my apartment and dancing to worship the Lord, something I do very often. On this particular day, I found myself dancing the way I used to dance when I was an unbeliever. As I continued dancing that way, the Holy Spirit said, "Dance to the Lord." I knew exactly what He meant. I stopped dancing and told the Lord that I was sorry. I had been dancing in a very seductive way, with my butt protruding out, similar to the way people dance in nightclubs. Who was I dancing to? Was I dancing to the Lord, or to please my flesh?

Do you see this kind of dance on God's altar? At the time, I was wearing a dress that looked nice to me. But frankly, it was only suitable for wearing indoors during the summer, or when one is alone with a spouse. It is no wonder that I found myself dancing seductively. I realized that as I had put on that dress, preparing to go out, the "old man," the "old Rhema," my fleshly nature was surfacing again. Once the Holy Spirit rebuked me, I quickly removed the dress and found something more appropriate to wear. What about you? How do you dress when you go out? Do you sometimes dress like a "street girl?"

God is concerned about everything, especially about how we look, and represent Him. He is concerned about our beauty. I have actually heard the Lord compliment me, saying, "You are a beautiful lady. Silver looks great on black people." Because of this, I only buy silver jewelry now. The only gold jewelry I have is my Star of David, and that is because I had already bought it by the time I received this beauty advice from the Father. God is indeed concerned about how we look.

CHAPTER FOUR

REVEALED IN PRAYER; BIRTHED IN PRAYER

Have you ever been in a church that is full of godly men and women who have sought the face of the Lord in prayer for the congregation? The Lord has prophesied mighty things about His church. He has unique plans for each individual congregation, like an open heaven. But, how is this open heaven going to manifest? When will the church experience all that He has in store for her? It is all a result of prayer; staying in His presence, praying. It will require sacrifice on our part; the discipline of calling on the Lord until all He has promised has come to pass. It is nice and easy to go to the Lord briefly at times to remind Him about His promises, but that is not enough. We will have to take some major steps if we are to see *major results*.

Here are a few:

- There must be repentance, which will mean weeping and groaning; whatever it takes.

- Forgiveness will have to follow.

- We will have to live in love, as the Lord commanded us.

- Serious corporate prayer with fasting; not just certain individuals praying, but everyone has to get involved. We, the body of Christ, are all called to pray, and to pray without ceasing.

- We must worship the Lord our God in spirit and in truth.

- It is necessary that we daily and prayerfully read and meditate on God's Word.

- Give thanks to the Lord, before, and after our prayers are answered.

Worship Is a Lifestyle

We need to be engaged in constant worship—not just on Sundays. *Worship needs to become our lifestyle.* We cannot experience instant revival, then after the service is over, go about doing worthless things expecting the revival to remain. We have to learn how to sustain the baby we are giving birth to—"revival." We want real revival that will grow and flourish, and be constantly evident in our lives, our homes, communities, workplaces, and cities. We want it to flow to the nations as we travel, carrying God's glory with us, Amen. We also need to learn how to experience and maintain the anointing; and how to remain on fire for Him in every seasons. That is why we have to get back into the Word of God and find out how our Master, Jesus, managed to succeed. There is no new formula. The Bible provides our example.

One day, I was reading the Bible. Every time I read about Jesus' lifestyle, I embrace everything about Him. As I read it, I paused and prayed, "Lord I want to be like you; to have the anointing you had."

"Nice and easy," He replied, "It is the same anointing".

Jesus is not selfish! He has given us everything freely, willingly withholding nothing. That is how we ought to pray for each other: wholeheartedly, withholding nothing. Develop a desire to be like the Lord; then ask Him to make your heart's desire become a reality. The Holy Spirit in us is the same Spirit who raised Him from the grave. I thank the Lord for His Spirit. I am so grateful. Where would we be without the Holy Spirit? Running around in circles, doing crazy things, I suppose.

> "*7 Ask, and it shall be given you; seek, and ye shall find; knock, and it shall be opened unto you: 8 For every one that asketh receiveth; and he that seeketh findeth; and to him that knocketh it shall be opened. 9 Or what man is there of you, whom if his son ask bread, will he give him a stone*" (Matthew 7:7-9)?

Whether or not we ask for His guidance, He is faithful and just, and always comes to our rescue. It is both polite and honorable for a child to ask of His Father who has all the answers. As we worship Him, let's give Him the honor and respect He deserves. Let's give Him our best. When you are in the assembly of believers, in church or a conference, don't focus on the person sitting next to you; focus on giving honor to our merciful God. Some casually stand with their hands in their pockets when they stand before the King of kings. Some have never humbled themselves or bothered to kneel down before their Maker. Oh someday He will break you and compel you to kneel and lift up holy hands in total surrender to Him.

Don't be ashamed of Him in public worship. If you feel you should kneel, go ahead and kneel. Lift your hands to Him, and express your love for Him. Letting yourself loose in a deep and intimate time of worship and prayer. Speak to your Father; sing songs of love and praise to Him. Do not hold back. Instead, make sweet melody to Him in your heart. God loves our worship. It's deep calling unto deep; yes, He loves it. Don't leave it to the worship team on the platform. *You* were created to worship Him. Open your heart and worship with other believers, lifting their voices in unison, and when it is time to dance, dance unto the Lord. Amen!

"A son should honoureth his father, and a servant his master: if then I be a father, where is mine honour? And if I be a master, where is my fear? saith the Lord of hosts unto you, O priests that despise my name. And ye say, Wherein have we despised thy name" (Malachi 1:6)?

I encourage you to find out more from Scripture how we are to worship God. You will discover that there is no set pattern or procedure, and even though some perhaps go overboard, or behave extravagantly in their expression of worship, the Holy Spirit still leads His people. Yes, there definitely are examples of "radical" worship in the Bible. Note the profound example of King David.

David, although a king, worshipped the Lord with all his might, publicly dancing to the Lord. He became so lost in his expression of awe and worship that he did not care that his royal robe had fallen off him. Even though he was the king of Israel, he did not restrain his very public act of worship and prayer. Was that a case of his being foolish, or showing off; or was it an example of his uninhibited praise to God? You answer that for yourself. Either we do it correctly, or we will go around "that mountain" for forty years, like the Israelites in the wilderness. Remember, many of them never made it into the Promise Land. It is so easy to please the Lord when we go to Him with honest, sincere, and open hearts. Let's bring out what we have mastered in our prayer closets, and together, as one body, worship Him, and revival will break forth.

God inhabits the praise of His people. What you do in the closet, when you are alone, should be the same as when you are in public. He will teach you how to lift your hands; how to bow down, to kneel, and when to lie prostrate. And yes, at times He wants you to dance for Him. As is often said, practice makes perfect. Feel free, and don't focus on what others may say. Be at liberty, because your Liberator, Jesus, liberated you two thousand years ago.

Once the Lord told me to "be an example." So, when it comes to worshipping Him, I let myself go and I totally immerse myself in His presence. The Lord keeps telling me to worship, sometimes He starts to sing and I join Him. He ministers to me intensely through praise songs, and He answers my questions by singing back to me. Then I thank Him, singing songs of love to Him, and we can go on and on till I fall asleep on the carpet, or on my knees, or when He tells me go to bed.

At the end of 2005, God confirmed to me that I had been going through stuff; I mean heavy-duty stuff. He brought me through, as pure gold. As I write this paragraph, I'm thinking about how, yesterday, I received some African tapes and danced, not knowing what I was doing. He complimented my dancing before Him. He told me, "It is important that you are dancing." There are certain things we do not understand. One of them is the impact that some prophetic acts have in the spirit realm. But God teaches us.

I do crazy things all the time, behaving like a fool for Jesus. My friends, it is high time we get back to His Word and learn from Him. Each time we do, He will reveal a different facet of Himself and His Truth to us. We are so blessed. God has made it so easy for us. The Bible has been written to guide and to serve as an example for us. You see, my friend, God is concerned about everything about us—especially how we worship.

If the angels bow down, and the elders who have already made it to heaven cast down their crowns, how about us who are still here? "Party" with the Lord your God—worship Him.

Why can't we fall and be fools for Him? I don't do crazy things to impress anybody, or to manipulate things. I do it to please my King. He has not complained yet. He loves it. If He didn't, He would have told me.

God is concerned about how you lift those holy hands to Him; how you become as a child and dance for Him; how you make crazy intimate sounds when you worship Him! Worship thrills God. Worship in tongues as a true worshipper. He is seeking those who worship Him in spirit and in truth. (John 4:23-24)

Never judge how others worship. Do you recall what the Lord did to King David's wife, Michal, when she criticized him for his unrestrained worship?

"14 And David danced before the LORD with all his might; and David was girded with a linen ephod. 15 So David and all the house of Israel brought up the ark of the LORD with shouting, and with the sound of the trumpet. 16 And as the ark of the LORD came into the city of David, Michal Saul's daughter looked through a window, and saw king David leaping and dancing before the LORD; and she despised him in her heart..." "20 Then David returned to bless his household. And Michal the daughter of Saul came out to meet David, and said, How glorious was the king of Israel to day, who uncovered himself to day in the eyes of the handmaids of his servants, as one of the vain fellows shamelessly uncovereth himself!

²¹ And David said unto Michal, It was before the LORD, which chose me before thy father, and before all his house, to appoint me ruler over the people of the LORD, over Israel: therefore will I play before the LORD. ²² And I will yet be more vile than thus, and will be base in mine own sight: and of the maidservants which thou hast spoken of, of them shall I be had in honour. ²³ <u>Therefore Michal the daughter of Saul had no child unto the day of her death</u>" (2 Samuel 6:14-16; 20-23).

God is concerned about how you treat His people. If you criticize, slander, gossip, and try to block others from ministering to the Lord by saying untrue things to the pastor or leaders of the church, it is an offense to God. He will fight for your fellow brother and sister. Leave it to God to expose a person, if He so chooses.

Keep your words to yourself if you cannot say something good. Do not open your mouth. Ask the Lord to set a guard over your mouth. Some people display immaturity and insecurity by not being able to keep their tongues from speaking evil about others. I remember one occasion when one sister approached me, with her helper, and rudely asked, "Are you going to bring your pretty face whenever we hold a meeting?" I simply smiled. She had only recently joined the ministry, had not been around for even a year. But already, she thought she ran the show. Time will tell, because the Lord knows the beginning and the end of all things. Interestingly, I saw this in the spirit before it happened, before she started working in this ministry. I was on a flight to Africa and received a revelation of it. I asked the Lord, "Why?" Do not allow envy to develop in the body of Christ, because it is the work of the flesh.

> *"Envying, murders, drunkenness, reveling, and such like: of the which I tell you before, as I have also told you in time past, that they which do such things shall not inherit the kingdom of God"* (Galatians 5:21).

The tongue is like a fire that burns so fast it is important that we ask God for wisdom when we speak. Some think they can put you to flight by their words, but I have learned not to allow people to hurt me with their unruly words. When it happens now, I don't defend myself. Instead, I worship and ask God to deal with the matter. I love Isaiah 6:5. Isaiah, the famous prophet, had seen the glory of God and the angels worshipping God. He had been totally exposed as he was confronted with the absolute holiness of God. In that moment, he received a revelation about his lips. Isaiah writes, *"Then said I, Woe is me! for I am undone; because I am a man of unclean lips, and I dwell in the midst of a people of unclean lips: for mine eyes have seen the King, the LORD of hosts."*

Verse one of that sixth chapter says that King Uzziah had died. We have to die to self and ask the Lord to do a work in us. He will speak to us and give us directions, but it is up to us to either carry on in our unrighteous way, or submit to Him by saying, "Lord help me in this area, and that area." It really is that easy. He will do anything for us. Now that is GRACE!

I anoint my tongue every day, desiring not to sin with vain words, words that wound and drive people from church. Remember, we will be judged for every idle word. Joking and jesting is another thing people often do. Then when they say something they realize they should not have said, they cover it up by saying, "I didn't mean it, I was just joking." No, you were not joking, because out of the abundance of the heart, the mouth speaks. The Lord gave me this word.

"And they shall fight against thee; but they shall not prevail against thee; for I am with thee, saith the LORD, to deliver thee" (Jeremiah 1:19).

I cried and sobbed when the Lord revealed the calling, gifting, and ministry He has appointed me to carry out. I thought of what Jeremiah, and what the Lord Jesus went through. But the Lord comforted me saying, "You have not suffered unto blood." Thank God, we do not need another savior! The trumpet has not sounded yet, so there is time. But we must redeem the time. As the Bible says, *"Today, when you hear the Spirit don't harden your heart."* It is always best to act immediately when He points things out to you. Your Father only wants the best for you; but, He will not push you against your will. However, I realize that in my case, it seems I cannot get away with anything.

Let's get back to the sister I was talking about. As I pondered her reaction towards me, the Lord told me to read Isaiah 54. I like the entire chapter, but verse 17 stands out for me. The prophet wrote, *"No weapon that is formed against thee shall prosper; and every tongue that shall rise against thee in judgment thou shalt condemn. This is the heritage of the servants of the LORD, and their righteousness is of me, saith the LORD."*

There is a big difference between you knowing the written Scripture, and the Holy Spirit Himself telling you about His Word. I cried when He gave me this Scripture. I could not stop sobbing. I read it again. The warning is right there. You better know who you are attacking or contending with in the spirit or you might catch fire. Worse still the earth can easily open up and swallow you. It has happened before with Korah and some of the children of Israel who contended with Moses. (Numbers 16:32) Why would we think it cannot happen again? What makes you think you won't be fired or replaced, just like the people whose job you took? Humble yourself, especially when you are in a new place, and honor those you meet when you arrive. They prayed you in and welcomed you.

Some don't like new people joining their team, because they are insecure, and feel threatened, or become jealous.

> *"6 For promotion cometh neither from the east, nor from the west, nor from the south. 7 But God is the judge: he putteth down one, and setteth up another"*
> *(Psalm 75:6-7).*

This goes for everybody from top to bottom, including the

pastor and the rest of those in the household of faith. HUMILITY! Right now, God is in the moving business. Like a government, He is reshuffling, placing everyone where He sees fit; so don't be shocked if He tells you to leave the church you have been in for years. Comfort zone or not, leave the country, go to the nations. It is not easy, but wouldn't you rather obey God? Obedience is better than sacrifice.

I just came from Uganda, where I attended the Open Bible Church in Entebbe, Uganda. I preached and taught on how to be practical about worship. They wanted the open heaven, too. Everybody entered a free atmosphere of worship so that the Lord could inhabit the praise of His people. Saints were on the floor, holy hands were lifted, some were jumping, some crying, some laughing; and they didn't want to stop. They didn't want any program or time limits when it came to worshipping the Lord. They allowed the Holy Spirit to have His way.

One Friday evening I went to the Renewal Christian Church in Lira, Uganda, where I taught on the same subject. The same thing happened, only more people were healed, delivered, even though no one laid hands on anybody. We concentrated on worshipping our Maker, and He touched His own people. Yes, worship can usher demons out. That is the easiest way, in fact. Demons cannot stay where Jesus is exalted and His holiness is constantly proclaimed. Lucifer and his agents will look for a dry vessel, one who doesn't praise the Lord constantly. That is the key—worship the Lord at all times.

A funny thing happened one day at my workplace. A

customer walked in, and instead of my usual "hello" in French or English, I blurted out, "Hallelujah!" *(The highest praise).* Everybody, including the customer, laughed. Because worship is such an important part of my life, worship is always on the tip of my tongue.

My understanding of the power of worship has increased. On my way to work, I had to park my car quite far from my workplace, which meant a long walk to my office. As I walked, I began praying and pulling down territorial spirits over the city of Vancouver. The Holy Spirit told me to just lift up Jesus. How do you lift Him up? Lift up in praise and worship. Never concentrate on demons, or the work of demons. Focus on the Son of God. Worship will drive them out. Sometimes when you try to help people, they can turn against you. When that happens, worship the Lord. Worshipping the true God clears the air, as they say.

Whenever I have issues that are disturbing to me, I worship Him. The Lord knows what disturbs me. Either the phone will ring, and someone will call me with an answer, or He will give me advice and a solution Himself. Sometimes I write out a list, lay it down, then play some music and lie prostrate on the floor in silence. I am expressing to Jesus, "I surrender. I can't handle this, you do it." What do you want from the Lord? WORSHIP HIM!

One day, the Lord asked me, out of the blue, "What do you want?" I was so stunned by the question, I did not ask for anything. Then I realized that I can still ask Him for what I want, and I began to do so. A profound thing happened as I taught a congregation a new song, *Say the Name of Jesus.* All the people had to do was respond, by saying, "Jesus." They were fast learners, who loved the Lord with all their hearts. We repeated the song over and over. It was clear that they did not want to stop. Eventually, I had to ask the associate pastor to come and close the meeting, since they had an overnight service to attend later, and some of them needed to go home before they returned to church for the overnight prayers.

After the service, a woman with a heart condition came to me on her knees to thank me for coming. She told me how she had been healed as we sang the song. When praises go up, blessings come down. That Sunday morning, it was hot—not with heat, but with the workout of worship and dancing. The turnout was great and the place was packed.

In Africa, there is no shortage of people to hear the gospel. One Sunday, there was an overflow crowd. Every chair was packed and people gathered to sit under the trees. I thought the time of worship was drawing to an end, and I should prepare to preach my sermon. But, then a different phrase would begin, and the singing would continue. In the African heat we sang, sweated, and wiped our faces. We sang, sweated, and wiped our faces. The more we sang, the more we sweated. The more we sweated, the more we wiped our faces. No wonder they still use handkerchiefs. Many needed towels to wipe away the streams of sweat.

It's no wonder why they experience such miraculous things in that part of the world. They routinely see miracles that many in the western church thinks stopped two thousand years ago. They have learned to maintain the anointing, keep the revival going, and to depend upon the

Lord. The good thing is, they listen and obey the Holy Spirit. They have teachable spirits, whereas Christians in some parts of the world think they know it all.

"Ye ask, and receive not, because ye ask amiss, that ye may consume it upon your lust" (James 4:3).

In addition, churches are different. For example, look at the account of the seven churches in Asia.

"1 The Revelation of Jesus Christ, which God gave unto him, to shew unto his servants things which must shortly come to pass; and he sent and signified it by his angel unto his servant John: 2 Who bare record of the word of God, and of the testimony of Jesus Christ, and of all things that he saw. 3 Blessed is he that readeth, and they that hear the words of this prophecy, and keep those things which are written therein: for the time is at hand" (Revelations 1:1-3).

You can read it yourself. God is concerned about His creation. He has placed in His church everything that anybody needs. All we need is to recognize the functions of each member, of the five-fold ministry (apostles, prophets, pastors, teachers, and evangelists) and utilize them under His leadership. Is it because we are waiting for an apostle, like John, a prisoner on an island to come before we will believe?

Ignorance will cost us a lot.

When you invite apostles to come to your church, you have to pay them, and buy their airfare, hotels, and food. Yet the one God appointed for your particular church is there, freely ministering to the congregation, but many do not want to listen to him or her. The church needs 20/20 vision—2 Chronicles 20:20 that is.

"Believe in the Lord your God, so shall ye be established; believe his prophets, so shall ye prosper" (2 Chronicles 20:20).

The Lord gave me a song as I was in His presence on June 9, 2005 at 3:57 a.m. I believe it is a universal song. I sang it to the church in Uganda to convey the message that the Lord gave. We must choose whether or not we will receive His revelation through His chosen vessel, even if he or she is not a high profile popular minister.

"18 I counsel thee to buy of me gold tried in the fire, that thou mayest be rich; and white raiment, that thou mayest be clothed, and that the shame of thy nakedness do not appear; and anoint thine eyes with eyesalve, that thou mayest see. 19 As many as I love, I rebuke and chasten: be zealous therefore, and repent. 20 Behold, I stand at the door, and knock: if any man hear my voice, and open the door, I will come in to

him, and will sup with him, and he with me. [21] *To him that overcometh will I grant to sit with me in my throne, even as I also overcame, and am set down with my Father in his throne.* [22] *He that hath an ear, let him hear what the Spirit saith unto the churches"* (Revelation 3:18-22).

We are only messengers. If you choose not to receive the message, you will not be rejecting the messenger; you will be rejecting the one who sent the message.

"For the priest's lips should keep knowledge, and they should seek the law at his mouth: for he is the messenger of the Lord of hosts" (Malachi 2:7).

Here is the song I found myself singing early that morning.

There is space to return x 2

There is space to return, return to me.

Yes, I will return x2

Yes, I will return, return to you.

There is a time to come x 2

There is a time to come, come back to me.

Now is the time x 2

Now is the time, to come back to me.

There is a chance to come x 2

There is a chance to come, come back to me.

This is the time x 2

This is the time, to come back to me.

There's hope in me x 2

There is hope in the Lord, come back to Him.

America comes x 2

America come, come back to me.

Then the nations will come x 2

Nations come, come back to me.

There is a place to come x 2

There is a place to come, come back to me.

Holy God x 2

Holy God, I will come back to you.

Pa-papa x 2

Pa-papa, I will come back to you.

This is the cry of the Lord's heart to us. Each of us needs to return to the Lord in every area of our lives.

"Return unto me, and I will return unto you, saith

the Lord of hosts" (Malachi 3:7).

I encourage you to read these chapters again - Revelations 1-3. There is a message for everyone. There is a message for backsliders, those who have lost their first love, who are watchers who are not standing watch anymore. They are those who wake up when they want; who are busy with life and don't have time for Him anymore.

America, Return to Me

If America would lead the way and be an example to the nations like in times past, it would not be hard for nations to return to the Lord. America must return and repent to the Lord. They are clearly leaders in the world. In return, the knowledge of His glory will fill all the earth. That is my passion—to see the knowledge of His glory fill the earth.

"… Holy, holy, holy, is the Lord of hosts: the whole earth is full of his glory" (Isaiah 6:3b).

"For the earth shall be filled with the knowledge of the glory of the Lord, as the waters cover the sea" (Habakkuk 2:14).

God is concerned about everything, especially about you returning to Him, rededicating your life to Him, and being anointed with fresh oil daily. Who will benefit the most when the knowledge of His glory fills the earth as the waters cover the sea? We will. That a man would die for his friend is extravagant love. Now He calls us His friends. He, the King of kings and Lord of lords is our friend, our elder brother. Amazing!

CHAPTER FIVE
A HOLY TEMPLE

Father God loves us very much. He is concerned about us. Like the old hymn says, *"What a friend we have in Jesus, all our sins and grief to bear..."* He cares when we grieve. He fully understands grief. As His Son, Jesus, was being crucified on the cross, He turned His face. He couldn't bear to look at His Son on the cross Who took upon Himself the sin of the world—our sin.

> *"From the rising of the sun unto the going down of the same, the Lord's name is to be praised"* (Psalms 113:3).

God is concerned about you 24/7. He is encouraging you to lift up your head. One day, at one of Dr. Morris Cerullo's World Evangelism Conferences, (I have attended many; and I am blessed each time I do.) I heard the Lord say, "Lift up your head." I lifted my head, stretched out my arms, and worshipped Him extravagantly. Suddenly all the weighty issues that were disturbing me were removed from off of my shoulders.

"Lift up your heads, o ye gates; and be lifted up, ye everlasting doors; and the King of glory shall come in" (Psalms 24:7).

"But thou, O Lord, art a shield for me; my glory, and the lifter up of mine head" (Psalms 3:3).

"... The joy of the Lord is your strength" (Nehemiah 8:10).

God is concerned when we leave our beds unmade. He is tidy. Look at the order and beauty of His creation. The universe declares His glory, and no amount of money can buy the fragrance of His presence.

"17 And the Lord spake unto Moses, saying, 18 Thou shalt also make a laver of brass, and his foot also of brass, to wash withal: and thou shalt put it between the tabernacle of the congregation and the altar, and thou shalt put water therein. 19 For Aaron and his sons shall wash their hands and their feet thereat: 20 When they go into the tabernacle of the congregation, they shall wash with water, that they die not; or when they come near to the altar to minister, to burn offering made by fire unto the Lord: 21 So they shall wash their hands and their feet, that they die not: and it shall be a statute for ever to them,

even to him and to his seed throughout their generations. 22 Moreover the Lord spake unto Moses, saying, 23 Take thou also unto thee principal spices, of pure myrrh five hundred shekels, and of sweet cinnamon half so much, even two hundred and fifty shekels, and of sweet calamus two hundred and fifty shekels, 24 And of cassia five hundred shekels, after the shekel of the sanctuary, and of oil olive an hin: 25 And thou shalt make it an oil of holy ointment, an ointment compound after the art of the apothecary: it shall be an holy anointing oil. 26 And thou shalt anoint the tabernacle of the congregation therewith, and the ark of the testimony, 27 And the table and all his vessels, and the candlestick and his vessels, and the altar of incense, 28 And the altar of burnt offering with all his vessels, and the laver and his foot. 29 And thou shalt sanctify them, that they may be most holy: whatsoever toucheth them shall be holy. 30 And thou shalt anoint Aaron and his sons, and consecrate them, that they may minister unto me in the priest's office. 31 And thou shalt speak unto the children of Israel, saying, This shall be an holy anointing oil unto me throughout your generations. 32 Upon man's flesh shall it not be poured, neither shall ye make any other like it, after the composition of it: it is holy, and it shall be holy unto you. 33 Whosoever compoundeth any like it, or whosoever putteth any of it upon a stranger, shall even be cut off from his people. 34 And the Lord said unto Moses, Take unto thee sweet spices, stacte, and onycha, and galbanum; these sweet spices with pure frankincense: of each shall there be a like weight: 35 And thou shalt make it a perfume, a confection after the art of the apothecary, tempered together, pure and holy: 36 And thou shalt beat some of it very small, and put of it before the testimony in the tabernacle of the congregation, where I will meet with thee: it shall be unto you most holy. 37 And as for the perfume which thou shalt make, ye shall not make to yourselves according to the composition thereof: it shall be unto thee holy for the Lord. 38 Whosoever shall make like unto that, to smell thereto, shall even be cut off from his people." (Exodus 30:17-38).

There is no fragrance like the Lord's. He visits when He wants, and sometimes leaves unannounced. On one occasion, He and I were enjoying wonderful fellowship, and after a while I grew tired. So, I went to lie down on my bed. As I did, He said, "Well, "bye-bye." Then, like a controlling wife says to her husband, I said, "Wait, *where are you going?*" He wanted to let me rest, which is fine; but I did not want Him to leave, so I sat up and said, "Don't go. See, I'm not sleeping. Stay." Funny. Don't you love Him? I do. God is fun to be with. He is always welcome, whether it is His voice, His holy fire, His breath, in visions, dreams, or the sweet fragrance of His manifest presence.

Come sweet anointing; Come, Holy Spirit.

Come, my Lord, anytime you want and don't leave;

Come, Lord, come; we your children love you.

He is clean, and He loves cleanliness. God is even concerned about how you smell. It is not worldly to use perfume. But, we do not have to mix all those spices found in Exodus 30:34. The blood of Jesus has paid the price for us, and He, the very Fragrance of the Father, is here with us all the time. Even in the bathroom as we shower, He will speak. He abides in us. The Holy Spirit is God. So anytime and anywhere, unannounced, we can experience the awesome fragrance of His presence.

"[18] For through him we both have access by one Spirit unto the Father. [19] Now therefore ye are no more strangers and foreigners, but fellowcitizens with the saints, and of the household of God; [20] And are built upon the foundation of the apostles and prophets, Jesus Christ himself being the chief corner stone; [21] In whom all the building fitly framed together groweth unto an holy temple in the Lord: [22] In whom ye also are builded together for an habitation of God through the Spirit" (Ephesians 2:18-22).

The Mexican Move

On January 31, 2000, I was on an assignment in Mexico with my son Emmanuel. We arrived, having made no plans or arrangements for our stay. Papa, Dr. Morris Cerullo, always makes hotel arrangements when we attend his conferences. I suppose I had become used to that. I guess I was in training, like an eaglet being taught how to fly. The Holy Spirit watches to see what we have learned. Normally I spend my holidays attending conferences, or accomplishing assignments the Holy Spirit assigns to me in my secret place of prayer. On this occasion, the command from the Lord was for me to go to the poor. I asked the Lord to be more specific, because the poor are everywhere, in every nation, including America. The Lord said, "Be in Mexico from January 1st to the 4th, 2001."

"What am I going to do there?" I asked.

"Take my glory!" He answered.

He is our glory. We are His "glory carriers."

"16 Know ye not that ye are the temple of God, and that the Spirit of God dwelleth in you? 17 If any man defile the temple of God, him shall God destroy; for the temple of God is holy, which temple ye are."
(1 Corinthians 3:16-17).

"For we are His workmanship, created in Christ Jesus unto good works, which God hath before ordained that we should walk in them" (Ephesians 2:10).

"The silver is mine, and the gold is mine, saith the Lord of hosts" (Haggai 2:8).

Everything I think I own is His anyway. He gives me grace, strength, and the ability to work. Honestly, if it hadn't been for the Lord being on my side, I would have been fired a long time ago—but that's for another book. Those who intercede for me can testify about that. Yes, the Lord is on my side, of whom shall I be afraid? I've seen Him turn my workplace into a better workplace. It's the same organization, but His grace abounds there because He is with me; and I pray it continues forever. God is concerned about your workplace too. Tell Him all about it. Do not stop or quit till He says it is over.

"1If it had not been the Lord who was on our side, now may Israel say; 2 If it had not been the Lord who was on our side, when men rose up against us: 3 Then they had swallowed us up quick, when their wrath was kindled against us: 4 Then the waters had overwhelmed us, the stream had gone over our soul: 5 Then the proud waters had gone over our soul. 6 Blessed be the Lord, who hath not given us as a prey

to their teeth. 7 Our soul is escaped as a bird out of the snare of the fowlers: the snare is broken, and we are escaped. 8 Our help is in the name of the Lord, who made heaven and earth" (Psalms 124:1-8).

I especially thank the Lord for His mighty men and women of God who lift me up in prayer to God. I value their prayers, because I know the power of prayer. It is one of the Master's keys. Jesus started with prayer and ended with prayer; and He still makes intercession for us. (Hebrews 7:25) Glory to God, He is with us—Emmanuel. I work and save money necessary to carry out the Lord's assignments for me. I wanted to get sponsors, but realized that could take years to accomplish, so I do it the way the apostle Paul did. He made and sold tents. My work also makes it possible for me to make mission trips He assigns to me. I rest in His presence; then I get an assignment; I take the assignment, and return; and the cycle continues until the Rapture.

We arrived in Mexico on New Year's Eve and the taxi driver took us to a hotel. My son was so tired and sleepy, I put him to bed, prayed briefly and left in search of a church where I could spend New Year's Eve. I do not speak Spanish, even though I plan to learn it one day. The receptionist spoke very little English, but managed to give me directions to a church.

On my way to the church, I saw a motel and decided to compare their rates with the hotel where I was staying. (We have to be wise.) My concern was, what if God tells me to stay in Mexico for a longer period of time. If so, I would need to be prepared for that. So, I stopped at the motel, glad that I had walked all the way instead of taking a cab. The receptionist led the way to the rooms and stopped, looked at me, and said, "That is a nice smell, what kind of perfume are you wearing?" Shocked, I thought; "What is he up to? He probably thinks I'm one of *those* girls."

I ignored him. He showed me the rooms, and on our way back to the lobby, he asked me again about the perfume I was wearing. That is when I realized that he might be smelling the fragrance of the Lord, for in those days, I didn't wear perfume, though I've recently started to.

I had left Canada at four o'clock in the morning, and by now it was almost eight o'clock in the evening. And, I knew it couldn't be a man-made perfume he was smelling. I explained to him that it was all about Jesus. "He is here with us," I told him. I explained further that spending time with the Lord will often attract a lovely fragrance. He was satisfied with my explanation.

Profound things happened on that trip that encouraged me to be instantly obedient to the Lord. While we were in Mexico we attended evening services. The church where we fellowshipped had evening services throughout the week, except for Wednesdays. Although the church was not far from our hotel, the nights were very dark. I didn't feel very safe on those streets after dark. We would walk back to the hotel from the church; and every night as I arrived at the entrance of the hotel, I could not move. God's holy fire would come upon me, and I would stand as though I were glued to the door. Emmanuel would be in front, watching me. *(He has become used to many odd things.)* The message I received from this was that this was the Lord's way of reassuring me that He was walking with us. Even in the dark, we are safe in His hands, even in faraway Tijuana, Mexico.

Inside our hotel room there were framed pictures hanging on the walls of the visions the Lord had previously shown me. I was so much in awe, I could not talk. I enjoyed the assignment so much, and to think that I had been reluctant to go in the beginning. I was like Moses, trying to talk God out of sending me. He had even told me that I would enjoy the assignment, and now I could see what He meant.

Now that I was in Mexico, I truly enjoyed every move of God. I experienced God in several mighty ways in that poor city. Many Mexicans I know despise Tijuana. When I tell them that I would like to return, they recommend other parts of Mexico. However, remembering how the Lord showed His glory in that town, I will go back someday.

The pastor even asked me to preach. I asked the Lord what message He had for His people. This was a time of profound glory, as the saints in the church worshipped and danced before the Lord with ready and open hearts. The pastor's daughter was my interpreter that day, and the Holy Spirit moved in a wonderful way, confirming His Word "mucho" *(much).*

Dear reader, never hesitate to go where the Lord sends you. My desire had been for the Lord to show me more of His ways, and He answered my thoughts. Our God is an awesome God, who knows our thoughts. Do not think evil.

Instead, repent of evil thoughts or you will be choked by the weight of sin. I know what I am talking about. I have experienced it; I have learned, and am still learning from Him, my mentor. People often ask what fragrance I am wearing. Sometimes when I'm at the "mountain of prayer," spending time alone with the Lord, He will come with this inexplicably sweet fragrance—very nice. Often, when I am by myself, neither praying nor singing, I sense his presence. I say, "It's you, my Lord," and I continue walking, or doing whatever I was doing. It is His way of assuring me that He is always with me. Oh! I love Him.

"Surely the righteous shall give thanks unto thy name: the upright shall dwell in thy presence" (Psalms 140:13).

"The steps of a good man are ordered by the Lord: and he delighteth in his way" (Psalms 37:23).

The Holy City

In 2000, we were in Jerusalem. It was my first time in Israel, and I was tired of being on the go so much that I did not have time to be alone with the Lord. My son was on this trip with me. For some reason, I was sad, something was missing and I felt like crying. Trips to Israel are usually a rush because the organizers sometimes try to pack everything into a few days. Days are spent rushing from one location to another; back in the bus to the next location; and you have to constantly keep up with the team. What some forget to include in these whirlwind tours is to set times to pray during the day. Apart from the short time of prayer at the Wailing Wall, all we had was a quick morning prayer.

Well, that was what I was missing for sure. I wanted some time alone, in the cool of the day, to be alone and pray. I decided to close my eyes in the bus and forget about sightseeing. The Lord knows how hungry and thirsty I get for His presence. I'm in love with the King of kings, and I never get enough of Him.

As the bus turned a sharp corner, the Lord came with such a strong, sweet fragrance, it was as if a bottle of perfume had spilt on the bus. He lingered for quite a while. That was the longest I had ever experienced the sweet smell of His fragrance. It is usually quite brief, a fleeting odor, which quickly disappears. But this time, I enjoyed the fragrance of His presence for a while, as did a sister seated beside me. That was all I had longed for—prayer and His presence, to make my day go smoothly.

The sister who perceived His presence with me rose from her seat to tell the other passengers; but none of them could smell the presence—only the two of us. I told her to come and sit down, that it was only a manifestation for us. She nodded and sat back down in her seat. No one was paying any attention to her. What was foolishness to them, thrilled, filled, and satisfied us.

He comes like the fragrance after the rain too; much like those that follow a sudden tropical African rainfall in the heat of the day as the sun reappears from behind the clouds. When one is sensitive to His presence, one can smell His fragrance, like a pregnant woman becomes sensitive to different scents in a way that they were not before they became pregnant.

Tune your thoughts to the Holy Spirit and be alert at all times. I sometimes imagine heaven, or building "a mercy-seat" for the Lord. The thought of His glory filling the sanctuary on a Sunday morning during corporate prayer is a constant prayer of mine. One day, after a trip to Africa, my African pastor asked me to take over and bless the people.

I neither speak fluent *Lango* (the language of Uganda's Langi people), nor can I read it. So, I preached in English, as a lady interpreted for me. During the sermon, she became "slain in the Sprit," falling to the floor, unable to speak. At that point, they gave me a second interpreter.

Two days after I returned from Africa to Canada, I was resting. I was wide awake when suddenly a white cloud appeared over me. It was an open vision. I felt a glorious peace and the presence of God encouraging me as a messenger of the gospel. The anointing, the grace, and the open doors He provided on my trip were astounding. How God does such amazing things is incomprehensible to me. I love Him so much.

We are promised a reward for preaching the Word of God. I love doing anything for Him. It's especially rewarding when you return, relax, and reflect on all He's done.

CHAPTER SIX

HE IS AN EVER NEAR GOD

God is interested, and wants to be involved in, every area of our lives—even the day-to-day mundane parts. One day, as I got up and rushed out of the house to go to work, leaving my bed unmade, He spoke to me that He was concerned with this part of my life. Yes, we have to work for a living, like the apostle Paul did, and sometimes we get caught up in the rush to get to work. I have seen some of my Christian friends expressing how they would like to quit their jobs saying, "The Lord said I should be in full-time ministry." While that might be true for some, I have seen many who go down this path eventually finding themselves in serious financial trouble, and end up having to look for a job again.

Be real! Who does not want to serve the Lord full-time? Even though it can be rough working at "secular" employment, it is a good idea to inquire of the Lord before you quit your present job. He calls us, and empowers us, to overcome wherever we are; which means He is concerned about your workplace as well. Talk to the Lord about everything. I am talking from experience because I have tested the water.

The good news is God can speak and calm the stormiest sea. Though working in some environments can be difficult, they can also be sweet times, seasons of testing, which will strengthen our faith, and prepare us for promotion to the next level and its battles.

Some ministers are called to full-time ministry, but some are in the ministry because they are too lazy to get up in the morning and go to work. We need to watch our motives for wanting to go into full-time ministry. Apostles, Prophets Evangelists, Teachers, Pastors and laymen who are serving the Lord with wrong motives should be careful. As Paul said in Philippians 1:15, some indeed preach Christ out of envy and strife; and some out of good will.

One day, I was praying about attending a particular meeting, and the Lord warned me to stop following vain people. Let us examine our motives for the decisions we make. Let us get back to our discussion about earning a living and still doing the Lord's work. If we all don't work, who will pay the tithe?

"For even when we were with you, this we commanded you, that if any would not work, neither should he eat" (2 Thessalonians 3:10).

We know that even though Jesus knew His calling, he worked with Joseph as a carpenter. However, He was being prepared, waiting for the appointed time. Remember when His mother told Him about the shortage of wine at the wedding in Cana, He said that His time had not yet come.

The same is true concerning God the Father? In Genesis chapter one, God created the heavens, the earth, and everything in it. He did good work, then He commended Himself. He saw the work He did was good. God is still working in us. Day by day, from glory to glory, He works to restore us to perfection, to our original status, which He created in us before man fell through our father, Adam. Thank you, Father, for the perfect sacrifice, Jesus, the second Adam.

> *"23 Man goeth forth unto his work and to his labour until the evening. 24 O LORD, how manifold are thy works! in wisdom hast thou made them all: the earth is full of thy riches"* (Psalms 104:23-24).

> *"But Jesus answered them, My Father worketh hitherto, and I work"* (John 5:17).

> *"And on the seventh day, God ended his work which He had made; and He rested on the seventh day from all his work which He had made"* (Genesis 2:2).

Allow me to revisit my earlier discussion about making my bed. One day, I got the shock of my life. As I climbed out of bed one morning, the Holy Spirit spoke to me through the voice of one of my pastors, Marilynn Culley, and told me to make my bed. From that day on, I have been disciplined about making my bed.

When I occasionally fall back to my old ways, He's there to remind me. One day, as I was lying down on the carpet praying, I had this vision. In the vision, I saw two beings with clipboards inspecting a room with three beds in it. My bed was in the middle, nicely made, and my headscarf was on it. In the natural world, there is only one bed in my bedroom.

What I learned from that experience is that I am not alone. It is important that we are careful about what we do in secret; because we are not alone. I believe the two beings who checked my bed were angels. That vision solidified my conviction that God cares about my neatness, and therefore I strive to make sure my bed is always neat. Ever since He warned about making my bed. We need His grace and mercy to see us through the day and night.

Oh, honor Him, reverence Him, He is faithful, true and just. Majesty, holy, holy, holy art thou, O Lord!

God is teaching me, preparing me for the future. Perhaps the man He has for me cannot stand an untidy helpmate. Our loving Father is the perfect teacher everyone needs. He is ever present to get us back on track, even teaching us the life-lessons we may have missed from our earthly parents.

There is hope for the future and the Lord gives us many opportunities to improve in every area of our lives. Truly, God loves us. Yes, He did instruct me about making my bed. Yes, God is God, He dwells in us, and He knows us inside out. Above all, He cares for us like a mother.

Sadly, some earthly fathers disappear from sight, leaving the responsibility of the welfare of their families, and caring for their children to their wives. The mother who develops a bond with her children through those nine months of pregnancy will do anything to care for, and provide for them even if the father is absent. When I say God is like a mother, I am not referring to gender. I mean He cares for us much like an earthly mother cares for her children. It reminds me of the lyrics of a popular song, "He is my everything." Do you recall how Jesus cried over the residents of Jerusalem?

> *O Jerusalem, Jerusalem, thou that killest the prophets, and stonest them which are sent unto thee, how often would I have gathered thy children together, even as a hen gathereth her chickens under her wings, and ye would not"* (Matthew 23:37)!

Don't remain sad if you lost your earthly mother. The Lord cares for you, like a mother. He is yours and you are His. He is forever your Father, He will never die and leave you missing Him, He is eternal, God Almighty. He has promised, "I will never leave you or forsake you."

> *"Before I formed thee in the belly I knew thee: and before thou camest forth out of the womb I sanctified thee, and ordained thee a prophet unto the nations"* (Jeremiah 1:5).

Talk to God about everything. Continue to ask Him questions, and He will tell you where to go, which route to take, and even what to pack. He will prepare you for every eventuality in life. Yes, He cares for you that much. Be an obedient child. Listen to Him when He speaks.

When I travel, I make it easier for the housekeepers, because I not only make my bed, but I also make sure the bathtub is easier for them to clean. That way, the cleaner or housemaid will not be cursing me as she cleans. I know it's their job, but put yourself in their shoes. Do unto others as you would have them do unto you. God is concerned about everything, especially about those who serve you, your housekeeper, and any service provider.

Remember the biblical episode about Sarah and her maidservant, Hagar. God rescued Hagar, who was a mere servant. Some of us are tempted to think we are superior to others, but never forget, we are all servants—God's servants. Plus, some hotel workers are Christians also, so be considerate to everyone. Who knows, you might even win one to the Lord through your kindness.

"17 And God heard the voice of the lad; and the angel of God called to Hagar out of heaven, and said unto her, What aileth thee, Hagar? fear not; for God hath heard the voice of the lad where he is. 18 Arise, lift up the lad, and hold him in thine hand; for I will make him a great nation. 19 And God opened her eyes, and she saw a well of water; and she went, and filled the

bottle with water, and gave the lad drink. ²⁰ And God
was with the lad; and he grew, and dwelt in the
wilderness, and became an archer"
(Genesis 21:17-20).

There's a lot in those verses, a sermon in itself. God opened the eyes of a maidservant, and protected her son from dying of thirst by giving her water from a well that had not been previously there. That was *supernatural* provision for Hagar and her son. It's as if the Fountain of Living Water Himself appeared. In fact, I believe that Jesus Himself *did* appear to Hagar, saving her and her son. Remember, salvation is for all. Single mother, rejoice! He cares for you and your children, He loves you. God is concerned about all people, whether they are Jews, Gentiles, Arab or whatever name is used to describe them. He sent Jesus for all of us. Ask the Lord to open your spiritual eyes so you can see in the spirit and discern rightly.

I'm in awe of the Holy Spirit. Sometimes, a thought will come to my mind that answers a question, provides a solution, solves a problem, or reminds me of something I must do before the due date—something like paying a bill. Yes, those little things. God is deeply concerned about us.

Living in tune with, and being sensitive to, the Holy Spirit is essential. I don't know what I would do without Him, nor do I understand how others live without Him. When I'm in His presence, talking to Him and do not get an answer, I will sometimes whine like a little girl, "You're not talking to me."

However, I know that if I will be patient and wait a little longer, He will eventually speak. He is my best Friend, on whom I can call anytime. He gives us a "direct line" to Himself, and no appointment is necessary. We just have to make time to get in His presence, and tune our hearts to hear His voice. He is always there for us.

Seek His face and totally trust Him. He will never gossip about you, or hurt your feelings; He is the Lover of our souls. He is adorable. He is everything to me, my Guide and Teacher. I long for Him, and call on Him at any time. He is not bothered at all, He is there for me. I suggest that you call on Him before you call a pastor. It's because pastors are human. They carry a lot of responsibility in running their churches, so they must also call on Him. Certainly it is okay to go to them with your problems when necessary; but don't burden them endlessly. Instead, rather spend time in your closet praying over the problems and issues that trouble you.

Praying In Obedience

One day, I was praying during my lunchtime at work, wondering why in spite of all my worshipping, praying and reading of the Scriptures, He had not given me the desire of my heart—a godly mate that I could treasure and love dearly. But I resolved not to push the Lord.

Knowing me so well, He said, "Hold your breath." Then He gave me a good idea, to "plant a seed." So, I called the ministry in the middle of my prayer time with Him. Lunchtime at work is my time with Him. I enjoy lunch in His presence, talking with Him and praying for whatever or whoever He assigns to me. I often skip lunch, choosing to spend the time in prayer, reflection and worship. When He shows me what He wants me to do, and then He repeats it, I know He expects me to act immediately. This is something I have learned over time.

God is concerned about what concerns us. He has promised to meet our needs; and to give us our heart's desires if we delight in Him. He knows what our true needs are. If He desires for you to be married, and you aren't yet, then be patient. My advice to people who are frustrated as they wait for a partner is, don't be bitter with the Lord. There must be a good reason why you are not married yet. Peace, be still, and know that He is God.

"Thou openest thine hand, and satisfiest the desire of every living thing" (Psalms 145:16).

"Lord, all my desire is before thee; and my groaning is not hid from thee" (Psalms 38:9).

"Thou hast given Him his heart's desire, and hast not withholden the request of his lips. Selah" (Psalms 21:2).

"Delight thyself also in the Lord: and He shall give you the desires of thine heart" (Psalms 37:4).

I once bought a very nice blouse that fit me well. When I got home, I tried it on and suddenly I began to itch. I was going to return it because I could not stand the itching, but the Holy Spirit told me to wash it. After I washed it, I put it back on and did not itch. I liked this blouse so much that I took it on my first trip to Jerusalem.

I took my ten year old son, Emmanuel, with me on the trip to Israel as well. I love my son dearly, and took him with me on this trip because I realized he would soon be in the higher grades at school, and I wouldn't want to pull him out of school once he reached the higher grades.

Emmanuel has traveled with me to several nations, and has been a great help because He is very sensitive to the Holy Spirit. Even better than that, he is a good friend. He is actually very mature in the Lord for his age. I am grateful to the Holy Spirit for mentoring him.

Before we left for our trip to Israel, I worked until the last minute, then rushed home to finish packing for the two of us. As I walked through our apartment, gathering all the things we would need, the Holy Spirit told me to clean Emmanuel's shoes. I immediately went to his room and found that his shoes had mud caked on them.

You see, God is as concerned about your children and their needs as He is about yours. He cares. They are His children. (God doesn't have any grandchildren.) He loves them. Often, when I worship and pray, He shows me faces of people He wants me to pray for. He even gives me the names of people for whom I should pray. They include children, adults, pastors, mighty men and women of God, government leaders and nations.

Merrilyn Culley

The amazing grace and love of God is intoxicating. One night in 1999, around 1:00 a.m., I was asleep when all of a sudden there was a sound of wild burning fire, and all I could see was a blazing fire. The vision I was experiencing was reminiscent of the burning bush that Moses encountered with yellowish red blazing flames, yet no smoke.

I awoke, and the Holy Spirit said. "Pray for Merrilyn."

I hastily slipped out of bed and onto my knees in the sitting room, which is my prayer room. I felt such an urgency to pray.

"Who is Merrilyn, Lord?" I asked.

He didn't answer.

Again I asked, "Father, who is Merrilyn?"

Still, no answer!

Thank God, that was the year I was baptized in the Holy Spirit, and prayer was, and still is, fuel to me. I was attuned to, and sensitive to the Holy Spirit's voice, much more so than before I received my prayer language. I began praying in tongues, and as I prayed, the Holy Spirit led me to bind the spirit of death. For five consecutive days, He awakened me at 1:00 a.m. and had me pray for the same lady.

I didn't know her, or what was happening in her life, but God wouldn't let me sleep. He was quite insistent. I kept asking Him who this "Merrilyn" was. In my mind, I thought it was Marilyn Hickey, the well-known Bible teacher. On the third day, He showed me the face of a lady with short hair, but it was not Marilyn Hickey. After the fifth day, the burden lifted.

The following day, one of the intercessors at church called and asked what I was up to. I told her I was preparing to travel to London, England for a spiritual warfare meeting. She said, "Remember to pray for the wife of Ernie Culley, the pastor of Glad Tidings Church."

I asked her the lady's name.

She said, "Her name is Merrilyn."

I said, "Wait a second, what's wrong with her?"

"She had a stroke," she explained.

I asked, "When did that happen?"

"Almost a week now," she said.

I said, "Wait, while I grab my notebook."

I checked, then I realized that for six nights the Lord had awakened me to pray for Merrilyn.

I told that to my friend, and said, "It is done!"

"Remove thy stroke away from me: I am consumed by the blow of thine hand" (Psalms 39:10).

As you read these words, pause and ask the Lord to remove all sickness from you and heal you. Praise Him, not the enemy who likes to see us afflicted with sickness and disease. Psalms 103:3-4, speaking of God, says: *"³ Who forgiveth all thine iniquities; who healeth all thy diseases; ⁴ Who redeemeth thy life from destruction; who crowneth thee with lovingkindness and tender mercies;"*

There's your anti-aging word. God cares.

When I returned from England, news had gotten around, and I was told that Pastor Culley wanted to see me. Somebody wanted to report the whole event, but I was reluctant for it to be broadcasted.

Emmanuel and I met with the Culley family, and we have been good friends ever since. Dear saint, we are a family from every tongue, tribe, people—a nation of priests. Today, Merrilyn is totally healed, and if she were not to tell you her story, you would never know how close to death she had come. She is special. God is concerned about all His children, especially Merrilyn, and not just Merrilyn, but you as well. You are unique and special, the apple of God's eye. Merrilyn's God answers by fire, surely our God is a consuming holy fire. Since having that experience, I am always encouraged to stand in the gap when the Lord shows me a face, or gives me a name. I immediately stop worshipping, or whatever I am doing, and pray till the burden is lifted.

One day, I was listening to Pastor Benny Hinn describe his function as a reed that carries the water. I asked the Lord, "If he is a reed that living water flows through, who am I?" The

Lord replied, "You should be the one who holds the reed in prayer." In addition to this, He has reminded me many times about my mandate, saying, "I have called you to pray for people. A few people form a clan; several clans form a tribe; and multiple tribes make a nation. Every nation, every tribe, every tongue combine to form a chorus." In one sense, of course, we all share that calling. When we abide in His presence, He will reveal important things to us.

"Call unto me, and I will answer thee, and show thee great and mighty things, which thou knowest not" (Jeremiah 33:3).

There is a reward in praying. We who minister in prayer benefit a great deal. There are cases in which we are life savers! We can alter the wicked intentions of the devil. There are many things God has called us to do. Never forget Paul's proclamation, *"I can do all things through Christ, which strengtheneth me"* (Philippians 4:13).

Prayer is an essential commodity for the Christian life and journey. Dr. Morris Cerullo often says the future belongs to the intercessor. Intercede! You will be amazed by what God shares with you, the nations He assigns you. Do you recall that He says in His Word, "Ask of me, and I will give you the nations?" He does not only give us the real estate of the nations, He also gives us the souls of the people in the nations!

"The fruit of the righteous is a tree of life; and He that winneth souls is wise" (Proverbs 11:30).

Is it raining too much? Ask Him to stop the rain. Is there a drought? Ask Him to send the rain. Is it too hot? Ask Him for cooler weather. Ask! Pray! Obey Him when He assigns those nations to you. Work with Him and He will position you, and give them to you. He may even send you to the nations. He is looking for women and men that He can show Himself strong in. The question is, will you go?

"And let us not be weary in well doing; for in due season we shall reap, if we faint not"
(Galatians 6:9).

One day, He said, "Argentina is hot." When you hear something like that, *what do you do?* Because of my previous experience, I started praying in tongues, the language of prayer. Whenever you are not clear about a statement you hear from the Lord, focus on what you know He said and pray in tongues until He directs you to pray in a language of understanding, or worship. You will find that the Holy Spirit starts to interpret what He has been praying through you to you. In other words, He is doing the praying and only needs your willingness or cooperation to accomplish the tasks on earth.

We need Him all the time; and He waits for our willingness. So, when you feel hopeless and when the enemy of your soul starts throwing fiery darts at you, ignore him. I heard the Lord say to me, "Consider this. I need you." As much as we need Him, He also needs us. He loves us and rewards us for partnering with Him—what great love!

Back to what I was saying about Argentina; as I prayed, He gave me wisdom to understand the situation and the condition Argentina was in. I started "seeing people" the way God sees them, and it became very personal. It was as though the people in Argentina were my blood-brothers and sisters.

You know what? If He entrusts me to pray for them, I'm honored to be found faithful to carry out the task. Because of Jesus' precious blood, we are brothers and sisters in Christ. Sometimes the Lord allows me to see, to feel, and even to smell certain things. He has blessed me with spiritual eyes and I'm thankful to Him for the wonderful gift of being a seer.

I encourage you to ask the Lord to give you what you don't have. He is the giver of every good and perfect gift. Do you lack any fruit of the Spirit? Ask Him, "Lord, I don't have much 'long-suffering.' I'm impatient." You will need that fruit someday, so why don't you ask for it ahead of time, and keep it in store for the time when you need it. That's when another fruit will prevail, a fruit called "peace." Peace will take you a long way. You need peace, it is essential! So boldly ask for all the fruit of the spirit.

Several times, He has shown me a huge tree with lots of branches with different fruit on them. Before I was filled with the Holy Spirit, I would find myself under this tree, but the fruit was not ripe, and then He would reveal to me that they were almost ripe. Gradually, as this revelation progressed, I found it easier to pray, after having been filled with the Holy Spirit, I found myself picking huge fruit; sometimes two or three at the same time, symbolizing the fruit of the Spirit, as they became more of a reality for me. (Learn more about the fruit of the Spirit by reading Galatians 5:22-23.)

Our Lord Jesus has spiritual eyes and which we need as well. Ask the Lord Jesus to open the eyes of your heart to see. Few things are as important as spiritual sight. Spiritual vision will enable you launch out into the deep and understand more about the Lord.

I recall the first sermon I ever preached in Aldergrove, British Columbia, Canada. There was a rehabilitation center there where a group of Kenyans held a Friday prayer meeting. A child had been miraculously healed there, and shortly after, they asked me to share something with the assembled group.

I went to Burnaby Mountain to pray and worship, asking the Lord what He wanted me to share. He said, tell them to "launch into the deep," and then He pointed me to Luke 5:5. That passage is where the Lord instructed the disciples to launch into the deep, because He could see in the spirit. He wasn't under the water, neither was He on the fishing boat. He was standing on dry land, but He could "see" in the spirit.

Prayer opens us up to this ability, but it does not come on a silver platter. As we grow deeper in our relationship with God, and prove ourselves faithful, over time it becomes easier. Sometimes the Lord allows us to see what the enemy is doing, or intends to do. Our assignment is to arrest it in prayer. Don't just rejoice because you can see, rather use the gift to serve the Lord and help His people.

I once saw someone die, what I believe now was a premature death. I say that because later the Lord showed me that I could have cancelled the spirit of death, and proclaimed long life to that person—someone's loved one.

May I offer this warning, however? As you are given eyes to see spiritual realities, beware of gossip. God will show you things to speak with Him about, not to tell others. This gift is not for gossiping. Never forget that the God who gives you eyes to see can also shut your eyes, and you will be blind again. Allow Him to open your eyes, and use that gift for His glory.

"Where there is no vision the people perish; but he that keeps the law, happy is He" (Proverbs 29:18).

"Now when he had left speaking, he said unto Simon, Launch out into the deep, and let down your nets for a draught" (Luke 5:4).

"Nathanael saith unto him, whence knowest thou me? Jesus answered and said unto him, before that Philip called thee, when thou wast under the fig tree, I saw thee" (John 1:48).

Open Your Eyes

I want to emphasize how important it is that you see in the spirit. If you are unable to see in the spirit, ask the Lord to open your spiritual eyes. Claim your right as His child. Read His Word, and claim that gift. Again, ask the Lord to open your eyes. He said, "Call unto me and I will show you great and mighty things." You may say that is just "Old Testament," to explain away your need to pursue it. However, there are many cases in the New Testament, like Saul, on his way to Damascus to persecute Christians. Both his eyes and understanding began to work accurately the instant he called Jesus "Lord."

How about the Apostle John, who saw wonders while on the isle of Patmos. He had quite a profound experience, didn't he? I don't know about you, but I ask the Lord lots of questions. He loves my questions. If He didn't, He wouldn't answer me; but He does answer me. This kind of relationship keeps us wanting more of Him, that's why we are well, and look so lovely. It is because there is One who loves us and has every answer.

Don't be envious of those who hear from the Lord, and certainly don't get in the habit of constantly asking them, "So you have a word for me?" You don't need a mediator between you and your Father. Jesus is the only mediator required. During His crucifixion, the temple veil was torn in two so we can boldly go before the throne of grace. Do not let someone be the one to ask for you. Get into the Father's presence yourself. He is waiting to hear your voice. In His presence is fullness of joy. You will discover great and mighty things you don't now know. You are His beloved child. He knows you by name. He is waiting for you to come and ask.

God is concerned about you coming to Him personally, He wants to fellowship with you; *yes, you*!

When He wants me to pray for people I know, Jesus calls them by their names or sometimes He just gives me a mental image of their faces, so I know who He means. It is okay to ask spiritually mature brothers and sisters to support you in prayer. Sometimes it takes a battalion to overthrow, or destroy an enemy camp. The truth is, these mature mighty men and women of God look to the same God for answers and have intercessors assigned to pray for them. Each of us needs prayer, and our spiritual leaders ask for prayers too.

How did they get to where they are? They did so by seeking the face of the Lord themselves, and not quitting. It is not always easy or pleasant, but it is always necessary. You have to discipline yourself, and make it your habit, your lifestyle. You may sometimes feel like you are in a dry desert land, and yet you know you are supposed to be like a strong, evergreen tree planted by the water. What do you do? Do you give up? Absolutely not. Do not even try or the enemy will take your eyes off the ball and make you grind your teeth in regret. The enemy's camp will throw a party and make fun of you, just as they did Samson. You don't even have to fool around with Delilah for the enemy to treat you badly.

Even if you have not crossed the line, the enemy will provoke you. Job had that experience and so did the Lord

Jesus in His wilderness testing. What did they do wrong? Nothing. They were targeted by the enemy because they chose to worship Father God. There is no turning back, once you have made it into the kingdom. There is abundant grace to see you through the dry season. So press on and fight for recovery. Deep calls unto deep. The Lord will assign His faithful intercessors to cover you in prayer, not the envious ones who call themselves intercessors, not knowing their works are exposed.

One day, I saw in the spirit a sister (who I knew) and her mother. After I saw that revelation for the third time, I approached them and nicely asked if everything was okay. They smiled and said, "We have been praying for you."

Surprised, I asked, "About what?"

"Oh, we have been praying that you would become a nun."

"Wow," I said. "Who asked you to do that?"

"Uh…" They couldn't say who.

I said, "Stop! The Lord wants me to marry. He has told me to pray for my marriage."

Sometimes you have to pray and cancel the thoughts and desires of others who are praying things contrary to God's desire for you. Please, if the Lord gives you a face or a name without specifying what the issue is, pray in tongues for them. If the revelations persist, pick up the phone, call and talk to them. They will open up and tell you what's going on. Don't assume, and pray something for them that is contrary to

God's will. The remnant of true intercessors is there, whether you know them or not, they will be praying for you because the Lord will assign your needs to them.

Trust the Lord! The Holy Spirit, who is in you, loves you. He's the best Intercessor; and He abides in us. Even when we think He is far away, He has not left us. Because He is in my heart, I sometimes put my hands on my chest and tell Him, "We are in this together." He will respond with something like, "We are in this together. You are winning. We will fight."

Read the back of the book—He has already revealed what the end result is for us. We win! The One that I love and trust is the only true God. I know whom I have believed and am persuaded that He is able to keep that which I have committed unto Him against that day. He promised He would never leave or forsake us, and He keeps His Word. He is faithful, true and just. His Word does not return to Him void. He assigns His ministering angels to minister to us. (Hebrews 1:14)

"11 For he shall give his angels charge over thee, to keep thee in all thy ways. 12 They shall bear thee up in their hands, lest thou dash thy foot against a stone" (Psalms 91:11-12).

You do not want someone else sleeping with the one you love to find out how good they are before you can have them, do you? So, get into His presence and experience His goodness. I heard Him say to me today, "I want you and I want to use you. Not anyone else but me." This is personal, and intimate; but it is not sensual. We are His sanctuary.

Once, on the third day of the fast, having had no food or water for three days, I felt weak. Feeling as if I knelt down, I would end up falling asleep on the floor, I got into bed so I could lie there quietly. Sometimes it's good to be silent. As I lay there quietly, the Lord said, "Talk to me." I immediately gained strength, got on my knees, and prayed.

You see, He understands our state. He is so kind. I felt wanted and important because the King of kings wanted me to speak with Him. I realized then, that as much as I long to hear Him speak to me, He also longs for me to talk to Him. Now that is a true relationship. Let your heart be His royal throne and let Him reign in you, surrender and obey. God is concerned about everything, especially you. He is ever so near, not a God that is far off, Amen. He loves you, yes, you. Don't doubt that for one minute. He loves you so much.

CHAPTER SEVEN
GOD OF THE NATIONS

The prayer of the believer is like a blazing fire. It is important that we take our assignments seriously, and being on time for our assigned watches, the times He wakes us up to pray. Those appointed times can vary, three o'clock in the morning seems to be a common time. I had that shift, and then I got promoted to one o'clock, which is a good time for me. I like to lie down once I've completed my assignment, and silently listen to what the Holy Spirit has to say. I have noticed that His assignments for me can come anytime there is work to be done. We've come a long way. He can rely on me to get the job done, and I totally depend on Him as we partner together on His missions. I do not say this to boast, rather it is to help you understand the nature and the demands of spiritual warfare.

That reminds me of my childhood. My mother was fond of calling my name to the point that even when she intended to call one of my sisters, she would call my name also, since I would respond to her calls immediately. Many times I would do other people's chores, and she liked my work, and my cooking. I learned a lot from her.

One of my mentors said that the Lord wakes him at four o'clock every morning to pray. I asked the Lord what time He wanted me to pray, and He replied that I should pray anytime, and to pray without ceasing. (1 Thessalonians 5:17)

Others have asked me what time the Lord wakes me up; well, I won't share that bedroom secret with you, it's intimate. It is like running a relay race. You get the baton and run your lap, then you pass it on to the next person.

If we all kept watch, both night and day, there would be fewer casualties and premature deaths. Perhaps that's why there are time differences between the nations, so we can take turns and easily keep watch twenty-four hours a day. Yes, we are to be salt and light to the world, and He wants to shine through us. We could have changed lots of things, events that should not have happened have occurred because the church does not keep constant watch. Do not forget, we are still in this race. Grab the baton, and take up the watch in your prayer closet, your corner, sanctuary, or secret place seriously. Then, pass it on!

Back to the experience about Argentina. In the previous chapter I shared how the Lord had told me that Argentina was hot. He was referring to a particularly intense heat wave that Argentina was going though. I was asking the Father to send cool rain to adjust the temperatures to prevent deaths due to the searing heat.

That was in May, 2004. Later, at a conference in September of that year, I met a brother from Argentina, and asked him about the conditions in his country. He informed me that in May, it had been extremely hot. Verifications like this encourage me to pray; because that's when the Lord reveals things we can stop from happening. You may ask then why He allows it to happen, is it to give us some work to practice on? Not quite. Maybe He sometimes gives the devil permission, so we can stand in the gap and fight for victory.

I typically ask what stronghold we are dealing with so I will know what, or how to fight. It's even better when He honors me by calling on me to carry out an assignment, or be the vessel to hold a nation, or save a life. He has not changed. He is the same today as He was yesterday, and He will be the same forever. He is still saying what He said to our father, Abraham, years ago; and what He told the early disciples two thousand years ago. He still says, "Go!" Tune your spiritual ears to hear Him and you'll hear many things. Trust me, you will not be able to keep up with Him. He loves to talk. Yes, God Almighty loves to talk. That is why I ask Him lots of questions. You see, I often do not understand. I have to ask Him, "What is that?" "What do we do now?" "Won't the enemy see us from here?"

The truth is, if we ask the Lord, He will blind and paralyze the enemy. You can camp at their gates, do damage, and return without being noticed. I call it God's KGB. Do you remember the story of Elijah and the Syrians? The Syrians thought Elijah was alone. That was also the case with David, when he went and cut part of King Saul's cloak. God has sent me on missions, and when I complete them, and get back, I am in awe. How did that happen and nobody noticed? He blinds the enemy.

Take Your Place

Ask lots of questions. Ask Him how you should pray and He will answer you. The disciples asked Jesus to teach them to pray, and He taught them what we traditionally call "the Lord's Prayer." What do you have to lose? He has the final answer anyway. So, why go through so much trouble and pain when there is only One with all of the answers? He is my shortcut. I love Him so much. There are many things to do in the Kingdom of God. There is no need to fight over any position, where to sit, where to stand in the worship team, or any other thing. The Lord Himself will position us. In winter, you dress warmly so you won't catch a cold. It's a winter season. But seasons constantly change. There are other seasons for you in the spirit. Patiently wait for Him to direct you since He knows the end from the beginning. There is a time for everything under heaven. (Ecclesiastes 3:1)

Recently, I was wondering what was going on in the spirit realm. I was faced with many challenges, but He has told me many times to never give up.

"I know the end from the beginning," He said.

"Be still and know that I am God" (Psalm 46:10). He is the Alpha and the Omega, the Beginning and the End of all things. Be strong and of good courage. Someone has to stand in the gap. Will you be one that He can trust and call upon anytime? Will you be one who will leave whatever you are doing, and do as He says? Will you?

"Son of man, I have made thee a watchman unto the house of Israel: therefore hear the word at my mouth, and give them warning for me" (Ezekiel 3:17).

Do you think He is only concerned about Christians? No, not at all. Jesus is concerned about both the saved and the lost. *"God is love"* (1 John 4:8b). I can relate to that. God loves me so much. He loved me even before I gave my heart to Jesus. I'm a walking miracle. I have almost been killed, but have seen the hand of God save me. All I can do now is thank Him, believe Him, and trust that all He promised me, He will do.

"We love Him, because He first loved us" (1 John 4:19).

I can give you the names of Hollywood celebrities. God loves them, regardless of whether you like them or not. He created them, and loves them. Some people get saved in ways that we would never have expected, because God has assigned His faithful intercessors to pray for their salvation. We will likely be surprised to discover that some unexpected people end up as our neighbors in heaven. The Lord sometimes shows me the faces of celebrities I am assigned to pray for. The Lord sometimes wakes me up to pray for leaders, even heads of state. He has ordained certain world leaders. Don't ask me why. Some we have asked for, and some we have voted into office. One way or another, they are in office for a purpose. God can use every situation or condition. He can even use the devil to accomplish His will and purposes, giving permission to the enemy to try to discourage us. When we emerge from these battles, our faith is strengthened. Remember the story of Job. There is a lesson to be learned in the book of Job; that book is in the Bible for a very good reason.

"6 Yet have I set my king upon my holy hill of Zion. 7 I will declare the decree: the Lord hath said unto me, Thou art my Son; this day have I begotten thee. 8 Ask of me, and I shall give thee the heathen for thine inheritance, and the uttermost parts of the earth for thy possession. 9 Thou shalt break them with a rod of iron; thou shalt dash them in pieces like a potter's vessel. 10 Be wise now therefore, O ye kings: be instructed, ye judges of the earth. 11 Serve the Lord with fear, and rejoice with trembling. 12 Kiss the Son, lest he be angry, and ye perish from the way, when his wrath is kindled but a little. Blessed are all they that put their trust in him" (Psalms 2:6-12).

He is working on all of us, the saved and the unsaved. There may be some you don't want to pray for, but He has taught me one thing—just do as He says. You must be a healed intercessor to be obedient to the Lord. Immediate forgiveness is essential. So, forgive right away. It does not matter whether who was right or wrong, forgive, so your prayers will not be hindered. This is very important. Forgiveness cannot be overemphasized. There will always be stumbling blocks, but they need to be dealt with quickly. Prophet Rick Joyner's book, *The Call* is the book to read. I won't say much more about this. You must learn to obey, because if He assigns you a task, He knows you are capable of doing it. Remember, we are His vessels. Never forget that He can call on somebody else if you aren't willing. You are not the only child on Straight Street. The choice is yours. He will even give you the assignment to pray for those who have persecuted you. This is another reason for us to forgive right away, when we are offended. I know it's hard, if not impossible, to totally forget the offense, but forgive anyway. (Matthew 5:44)

Paul persecuted the church, not knowing he was touching the apple of God's eye. You can read the story in Acts chapter nine. Ananias almost refused to go and heal Paul, for He was afraid. He and many others had not forgotten what Paul had done to other believers before the Lord struck him with blindness. One thing I know is this. When the Lord assigns us a task; He will be with us until it is completed. Just obey His instructions and do as He says. At times like these, I pray, "Lord, use them like Paul." That pays off, don't you think?

"For God so loved the world, that He gave his only begotten Son, that whosoever believeth in Him should not perish, but have everlasting life" (John 3:16).

We should not judge others. Leave that to God. The best we can do is pray that the Holy Spirit convicts them, and that they will receive Jesus as their only Lord before God takes breath from them.

Pray that they will *"... taste and see that the Lord is good..."* (Psalm 34:8b)

God's Word *"...is quick and powerful, and sharper than any twoedged sword, piercing even to the dividing asunder of soul and spirit, and of the joint and marrow, and is a discerner of the thoughts and intents of the heart"* (Hebrews 4:12).

> *"The heart is deceitful above all things, and desperately wicked: who can know it"*
> (Jeremiah 17:9)?

Only God knows the heart of a man, saved or unsaved. So, pray His Word so the Holy Spirit can correct the thoughts in a man's heart. Pray that God's Word will judge and correct believers around the world. He is Lord of lords. Be like father Abraham, interceding for Sodom and Gomorrah. Imagine that Lot your cousin is in Sodom or Gomorrah, and intercede wholeheartedly for the unsaved. The fact is, we are all related in Adam from the beginning.

> *"²⁶ And God said, Let us make man in our image, after our likeness: and let them have dominion over the fish of the sea, and over the fowl of the air, and over the cattle, and over all the earth, and over every*

creeping thing that creepeth upon the earth. [27] *So God created man in his own image, in the image of God created he him; male and female created he them"* (Genesis 1:26-27).

God is Concerned about the Salvation of Mankind

God is concerned about everything and everyone, especially you. He even loves, and Christ gave His life for those we think are wicked. We are all in the same boat. Some of us have been saved a little longer than others, but be patient and pray them in. I still do. I've literally cried before, praying that God will give me souls lest I die. Does that sound strange? I will go to a place where I am alone and mourn for souls.

One day, I went to Burnaby Mountain in Vancouver, where I often go and worship, singing my heart out. Actually, I learned to sing up there, and the Lord has done great things for me up on that mountain. That particular day, I went to a different spot in the woods and started to lament and cry, "Lord, give me souls."

Eventually I finished praying and dried my tears. As I emerged from the woods, there were two girls and a boy waiting for me. Don't ask me how they knew I was in the woods. All I can say is that prayer work. In fact, as I arrived, the two girls said, "We have been waiting for you." Pointing to the boy with them, they continued, "We have been trying to tell this friend about Jesus, and we are getting nowhere. Could you help us?"

Oh! That was an instant answer for me. No tears wasted. The boy gave his life to Jesus, and we asked the Lord to fill him with the Holy Ghost. These were foreign students who had come to Canada to study English. But they got a greater reward for their efforts to pursue their educations. They received Jesus. To top it off, they are obviously going to take the testimony of Jesus back to their nation.

I came home so happy. Some days it is easy, as if the ocean tides have brought all the fish ashore. On other days, it is like a dry and barren land, in which we thirst for God to move in His might. It is an abundant life. That is why He came, that we may have life. God is concerned about everything, especially about all of us. We are all special in His eyes. He loves you. God is concerned about strangers, and about foreign students, so be kind to them. Offer them directions when they don't know your city, and when the time is right, offer them directions to heaven.

CHAPTER EIGHT
HEALING IS THE CHILDREN'S BREAD

The Lord is gracious and compassionate; slow to anger and rich in love. He is good to all. Once, in the course of getting ready to go to Israel, we needed a new suitcase, so I went to Sears. But I thought the prices there were too high. I did not even try The Bay (a popular Canadian department store) because, most of the time, The Bay is more expensive than Sears. I went to downtown Vancouver, to my bank branch, and while I was there, I felt nudged to check on the suitcases at The Bay. When I got to the suitcase section, I asked for help because there were two prices for the same kind of suitcase.

I called the sales clerk over and she was not very nice. She walked past me with that "You can't afford it" look. *Some clerks!* So, I waited for a sales clerk who was busy serving another customer to finish. He was very kind, and after chatting with him, I found out that he too is a Christian. We talked about Israel, and I found out that he had also been to Israel. He was really helpful and happy that I was going to Israel. The price of one suitcase was $248.99; while the other one was $60.99. They were the same size and brand. I'm sure you can guess which one I purchased. The Lord had taken me to The Bay, and blessed me with an *American Tourister®* suitcase for $188 dollars less. Glory to God!

"The steps of a good man are ordered by the Lord: and He delighteth in his way" (Psalms 37:23).

My niece, Leslie, loves to lead devotion with a chorus that says, *"My God is so big, so strong, and so mighty, there is nothing my God cannot do."* God is concerned about everything, especially about you and your kids.

My Son

I love to share about my son, have you noticed? He is my friend, my prayer partner, mission companion, and a good advisor. At the age of eight, he was baptized in water, and was filled with the Holy Spirit at the age of nine. In Matthew 19:14, Jesus said, *"Suffer the little children to come unto me."* Some churches would not allow that, but I prefer to pay heed to what Jesus said, not men, how about you? I am his mother. I mentor him, and I know his needs. The Holy Spirit didn't object to filling him, so why would anyone else's opinion matter? Emmanuel is full of visions, revelations, and he loves the Word of God.

"And it shall come to pass afterward, that I will pour out my spirit upon all flesh; and your sons and your daughters shall prophesy, your old men shall dream dreams, your young men shall see visions" (Joel 2:28).

The Lord has blessed me. Emmanuel is a very understanding and obedient son. I give thanks to the Lord for him. He developed asthma at an early age, which became serious by the time he was four years of age. Being a single mother who worked night shifts then, it was very hard on Emmanuel; and even harder on me. I knew that he could stop breathing anytime, and I might not be near him to help. It made me sad to think of it. I bought him all the medication he needed, but the thought of my son puffing asthma medication really bothered me.

I hate sickness! I do not like pain, or any kind of discomfort. The fact that I had to take my son to a babysitter for the night; then pick him up early in the morning, and drop him off at school; and be with him only in the evening for a short time bothered me a great deal. I had no way out, but to ask the Lord to heal Emmanuel. From Sunday night to Thursday night, Emmanuel and I would not see much of each other. Come Friday afternoon, we were happy to be together until Sunday evening.

One week after cleaning up and doing our laundry, I had a free Saturday, during which I stayed in bed and sang to the Lord. I would only get up to give Emmanuel his breakfast and help him with what he needed. He would then go and play, and I would continue singing all the hymns I knew. When we prayed, I would tell Emmanuel to ask the Lord to heal him from asthma.

One day, I had a dream that I was in the kitchen and was going to my bedroom where Emmanuel was sleeping. He used to share my bed because I was afraid that if he was in his room, I wouldn't be able to hear him struggling to breath. In my dream, as I entered the bedroom, there was a being coming through the bedroom door. I asked, "Are you an angel?"

The angel nodded in agreement. He was the same height as Emmanuel, a little angel. Well, I have seen huge, tall, muscular angels. I told this little angel, "Please tell God to heal my son." The angel nodded in reply, and left. I went into the room where Emmanuel was lying on the bed. That was the end of my dream.

We continued to pray for healing. One day, the Lord instructed me to take Emmanuel for a physical checkup. I did not normally take him for checkups. I can't remember why, perhaps it was the doctor's words to me that Emmanuel would probably outgrow asthma at the age of seven, as he got older and involved in playing sports. Be careful about people's words, because they can cripple you. Now I listen to what the Holy Spirit says. Things may look contrary to what you believe, but always stand on the counsel of the Lord.

Whose report are you going to believe? Believe the report of the Lord. Men will tell you that there are giants in the land, and that you look like a grasshopper, but don't believe that, or you may miss your blessing. They may say, "There are several women around that man." Well! You're the chosen one. God said, "You are the only one who fits his rib." So be strong and go get your blessing, I am encouraging myself now.

One weekend, Emmanuel woke up, and the first thing he said was, "Mommy, Mommy, Jesus has healed me."

I asked him, "How do you know?"

He said, "Jesus came and healed me."

I said, "Oh!" I believed the moment he mentioned Jesus' name.

Emmanuel and I were so excited. I called the clinic and made an appointment to have him examined. At the clinic the doctor asked us the purpose of our visit. I told her we were there to check and see how Emmanuel was doing, so she got a stethoscope, examined his chest, and said, "His chest sounds good, there is no wheezing at all."

The doctor sat down and asked me what had happened. She had said earlier that he would possibly grow out of it as he became involved in sports. I told her about my dream, God's intervention and miracle. She knows I believe in God healing His people. She replied, "I have heard of things like that happening. I am happy for you."

So, she officially took my son off his asthma medication. To this day, Emmanuel has not suffered any asthmatic attacks. He runs fast and plays soccer without any breathing issues. I am so grateful to the Lord for healing my son, because he loves playing soccer.

When you find yourself in a similar situation, or worse, I encourage you not to give up hope, to persist in prayer, and to wait and see what the Lord will do. Yes, it is God's absolute will that we are one hundred percent healed. God is concerned about you, and your children's health and wholeness.

"He sent his word, and healed them, and delivered them from their destructions" (Psalms 107:20).

Do not be deceived. God loves you so much. He has no interest in destroying you. He wants you whole. He is *Jehovah-Shalom*, the Lord your peace; and *Jehovah-Rapha*, the Lord who heals you. It does not matter what the name of that disease. The AIDS virus, cancer, and other deadly diseases are no match for our Lord. He is the healer of all sickness and disease. He can give you a new heart. Our God is the God of the impossible! What man failed to do, God can do, because He is the Creator God! Trust the Lord at all times. He is able to do exceedingly abundantly above all that we ask or even think. God is concerned about you.

"¹ Bless the LORD, O my soul: and all that is within me, bless his holy name. ² Bless the LORD, O my soul, and forget not all his benefits: ³ Who forgiveth all thine iniquities; who healeth all thy diseases; ⁴ Who redeemeth thy life from destruction; who crowneth thee with lovingkindness and tender mercies" (Psalms 103:1-4).

I am not suggesting that you go ahead and abuse the temple of God (your body), and expect Him to heal you. He might heal you, but do not put the Lord your God to the test. Honor and respect your body, and know that we are created in the likeness and the image of God, and His Spirit dwells in us. We are of great value, bought by a high price, the blood of Jesus. Jesus, the perfect Lamb of God, was sacrificed for us, purchasing us for God that we might become His prized possessions. Lamb of God, worthy is Your name, Jesus. Friend, surrender and dedicate your body totally to the Lord, and you will discover that He will sustain and protect you from every evil temptation. Ask Him to deliver you from the evil one. He is faithful and just to cover you under the shadow of His wings. He will hide you in Himself, so trust Him.

One thing I have learned is that I am not my own. So, I dedicate who I am and all that I have to Him. Whether it is money, my job, or anything else I have, I have learned to dedicate all to the Lord Jesus. I learned this after I suffered a great loss. The Holy Spirit would give me specific instructions regarding what to pray about, so that terrible events, including bloodshed, could be prevented. Believe it. The Lord works and fights battles for us. He will assign His children to pray and fast for us, and assign His angels to work on our behalf. Intercessors would call or write to me to confirm what He had told them to pray about. He has done great things for me, and is not finished with blessing me. We have many testimonies about His divine healing. So, the minute you feel strange, weak, or sickly, rebuke sickness and tell it to go, in Jesus' name. Do not give it time to land, and settle in God's holy temple (your body). Lay hands on your body and pray in the name of Jesus. You may remember how King David encouraged himself. (1 Samuel 30:6b)

> *"Submit yourselves therefore to God. Resist the devil, and He will flee from you"* (James 4:7).

If the sickness persists, call other believers and ask them to continue to pray for you. This is why the Scripture encourages us to call the elders of the church when we are sick or have a need.

> *"14 Is anyone among you sick? Let him call for the elders of the church, and let them pray over him, anointing him with oil in the name of the Lord. 15 And the prayer of faith will save the sick, and the Lord will raise him up. And if he has committed sins, he will be forgiven"*
> (James 5:14-15, NKJV).

Corporate prayer—or the prayer of agreement—is powerful. Even if you are caught unawares, like Job, reach out to the Lord and to other members of the Body of Christ. Do not suffer alone. Since I do not like pain and suffering, I usually ask the Lord to heal me quickly whenever I feel I am being afflicted with sickness.

"Heal me, O Lord, and I shall be healed; save me, and I shall be saved; for thou art my praise" (Jeremiah 17:14).

That is a powerful statement from the prophet Jeremiah that we can use. I remind the Lord about His Word, and speak the Scripture into my situation. I take it that He is literally talking to me. More than that, I *know* that His Word is for me, and that the Bible was written for our example and encouragement. The Scripture is a wonderful treasure that makes life easier. There is a chorus that I sometimes sing that says,

"I have a wonderful treasure,

The gift of God without measure,

We will travel together,
My Bible and I."

Meditate on the Word of God. Store it in your heart, and speak it to the circumstances in your life to encourage yourself.

"This book of the law shall not depart out of thy mouth; but thou shalt meditate therein day and night, that thou mayest observe to do according to all that is written therein; for then thou shalt make thy way prosperous, and then thou shalt have good success" (Joshua 1:1).

Learn from our master Jesus, who quoted the Scripture to the devil, and used the phrase "It is written..." to overcome the devil's devices.

> *"For the word of God is quick, and powerful, and sharper than any two-edged sword, piercing even to the dividing asunder of soul and spirit, and of joints and marrow, and is a discerner of the thoughts and intents of the heart"* (Hebrews 4:12).

> *"In the beginning was the Word, and the word was with God, and the Word was God. He was in the beginning with God. All things were made by Him; and without Him was not anything made that was made"* (John 1:1-3).

Religious people, those who do not understand, say that Jesus came 2,000 years ago. But we know from the Scripture above that He has been here from the beginning. Jesus, the Living Word of God, is powerful. Meditate and memorize the written Word, speak it into your circumstances in the name of the Living Word of God, Jesus! Claim the blood of Jesus.

Utilize both the Old and New Testaments. Many people don't like to read the Old Testament. They don't feel it applies to them. But it is God's inspired Word, and God intends to use it in our lives. When my mentor, Dr. Morris Cerullo, started sending me yearly calendars with daily Bible readings starting from Genesis, I found that most of the inspiring quotations we use are found in the Old Testament. I started loving the whole Bible, kissing my Bible, knowing that my *entire Bible* is God's Word.

Often, when I finish a time of Bible study, I hug and kiss the Scripture, God's "love letter" to me, to demonstrate my love for Him. I so treasure the Word of God that at work, on my break, I do not hesitate to read it. Whether I am on a coffee break, in the bus, or on the train, I read it. It is a valuable resource. Read it with all your heart, as often as you can. One morning, in my bedroom, I found myself saying aloud,

"Lord, I love all of your Word."

The Lord answered, "Me, too."

Friend, love Jesus and keep His Words.

"Jesus answered and said unto him, If a man love me, he will keep my words: and my Father will love him, and we will come unto him, and make our abode with him. He that loveth me not keepeth not my sayings: and the word which ye hear is not mine, but the Father's which sent me" (John 14:23-24).

Some people complain that they cannot hear God. My first question is, "Are you born again?" My second question is, "Do you spend time in God's Word." If so, He will speak to you. In John 10:27a, He said, *"My sheep hear my voice…"* Listen sincerely, with a pure heart and clean hands, and He will make sure you hear Him clearly. (Psalm 24:4) I love to hear God speak so much that I will do anything to hear His voice. Even when He has spoken to me, I want to hear more. So, after worshipping Him, I pray, and then I wait for Him to speak again. Sometimes He puts me to sleep and speaks to me in a dream or vision. But because of my insatiable desire for His presence, I am never satisfied. Then I dig into His Word, and He reveals Himself powerfully, speaking more and more. *Read the Word!*

"Study to show thyself approved unto God, a workman that needeth not to be ashamed, rightly dividing the word of truth" (2 Timothy 2:15).

The songs we sing and the prophecies that the Holy Spirit gives us should align with the Word of God. The Lord will never say something to us that contradicts what He has written. Precept must be upon precept, and line upon line.

"11 For with stammering lips and another tongue will he speak to this people. 12 To whom he said, This is the rest wherewith ye may cause the weary to rest; and this is the refreshing: yet they would not hear. 13 But the word of the Lord was unto them precept upon precept, precept upon precept; line upon line, line upon line; here a little, and there a little; that they might go, and fall backward, and be broken, and snared, and taken. 14 Wherefore hear the word of the

Lord, ye scornful men, that rule this people which is in Jerusalem" (Isaiah 28:10-14).

I was at the hospital on July 17th, 2005 visiting some members of our church, knowing that the enemy was attacking on all fronts. But we serve a mighty God who is always with us. He is not a "far off God." He is very near to us. He *lives in us!*

"Am I a God at hand, saith the Lord, and not a God afar off" (Jeremiah 23:23)?

Innocent children are being attacked by the enemy, as he tries to destroy and bombard their parents with worry for the lives of their children. But we should always remember that God is concerned about our children. He loves and cares for them! If your child is sick today, fight for their healing. Ask the Lord to heal them, and He will. Call upon the Lord your God. Persist until you get your breakthrough. You may have to fast. Whatever it takes, *just do it!*

Some parents fold their hands, comfort themselves, and say, "If it's God's will to heal my child, He will." Yes, it is God's will to heal. It is also appointed for everyone to die. (Hebrews 9:27) But no one should die prematurely. Do not give up praying for your children or loved ones. Is he or she on drugs? The Lord is well able to deliver them. Pray intently, ask others to pray. Your prayers will activate God's power to get them off drugs. Are they on the streets? Call on the Lord. Don't sit in silence. Pray! God is concerned about them, and He is faithful and just, and will answer you.

"20 Now unto him that is able to do exceeding abundantly above all that we ask or think, according to the power that worketh in us, 21 Unto him be glory in the church by Christ Jesus throughout all ages, world without end. Amen" (Ephesians 3: 20-21).

"For Zion's sake will I not hold my peace, and for Jerusalem's sake I will not rest, until the righteousness thereof go forth as brightness, and the salvation thereof as a lamp that burneth"
(Isaiah 62:1).

CHAPTER NINE
EMERGENCY LINE

I did not know there is an "emergency line" in heaven until my beloved sister was at the point of death. Those were days of intense prayer, and days of discovery. The Lord is waiting for us to persistently call on Him so He can reveal mighty things to us. His Word to us is:

> *"Call unto me, and I will answer thee, and show thee great and mighty things, which thou knowest not"* (Jeremiah 33:3).

I have a lot of responsibility and obligations concerning the care of my relatives in Africa. It's actually quite common with many African immigrants who live in the West. In 2002, I lost one of my younger sisters. She had three kids, so I became responsible for their upkeep, in addition to looking after my son, Emmanuel. In effect, I became a single parent with four kids. I thank God that He has given us the mind of Christ Jesus, because without His wisdom, we would collapse under the weight of life's obligations. God is so merciful!

When I learned later that two of my sisters had become ill, having been diagnosed with AIDS, I desperately wanted to go home and lay hands on them to pray for them. I had not been back to my native Uganda since the 1985 coup. I felt strongly that if I went home, God would release His healing power to my sisters through me. He has done this for others, through my praying for them over the phone, and has helped many as I laid hands on, and prayed for them. I knew that He could do the same for my sisters. I felt it was their turn to be touched and blessed by Him.

The more I thought about the situation, the angrier I became at the damage that sickness was afflicting on my people, not just the AIDS virus, but also cancer and leprosy. I hated the fact that many in my family back in Uganda were trapped in Islam, and others were idol worshippers. In view of this, I decided to go on a forty-day fast. In the middle of the fast, a friend called and said, "Rhema, the Lord has asked me to pray and fast for you for three days."

"What did He ask you to pray for?" I asked.

She listed about seven different topics, and I agreed to join her in prayer about them. We agreed not to call each other until the three days had passed. After three days, she called me and confirmed the things that were bothering me, including my desire to go to Africa to see my family.

I continued with the fast, and the Lord revealed to me what He was going to do.

"Islam is coming down," He said. "Regarding your two sick sisters, I AM going to heal them; you mentor and pray for them."

The Lord ministered and blessed me and I got so excited. I called my sister Fatuma to tell her the news. She encouraged me more when she told me that earlier, the Lord had given her this Scripture.

> *"⁴ Surely he hath borne our griefs, and carried our sorrows: yet we did esteem him stricken, smitten of God, and afflicted. ⁵ But he was wounded for our transgressions, he was bruised for our iniquities: the chastisement of our peace was upon him; and with his stripes we are healed"* (Isaiah 53:4, 5).

I could feel God's power in this young believer and could see how merciful our God is! Her husband had already died from AIDS, and now the Lord was sparing her life. What amazing grace! I told my sister, "You are healed." It was good to encourage her that way because she had all the symptoms of death. She had developed growths in her throat, making it difficult for her to breathe. Her legs were swollen, she had wounds, and it was very difficult for her to walk. I kept encouraging her, saying that she was healed, and assured her that I was coming to see and pray with her.

The Lord showed me in a vision how I flew up, like a bird, and saw my sister seated helplessly. In the vision I flew down, touched her and continued flying. I sensed that it symbolized a trip to Africa. On the phone, we prayed about her throat, and the growths disappeared. Every day I called to give her the Word, and to pray with her. The day after we prayed about the growths, I asked her:

"How is your throat?"

"Oh! The growths are gone!" she replied.

Praise God. In addition, I would ask if she had any prayer requests, and once she gave me those requests, I would pray with her, and give her a Scripture for the day. Then I would call her the following day. As regular as clockwork, anytime I called after praying over an issue, she would confirm that the problem had been resolved. Also, we prayed for more than just physical healing. She had family issues to deal with. With her husband dead, and her in-laws fighting over his inheritance, we prayed about many things. God answered our cry, and the Lord came through for Fatuma regarding the inheritance. She received what she wanted. Yes, God is able. He gives favor. This pattern of praying on the phone, and confirming God's answers to our prayer went on for almost a month until I made arrangements and went to Uganda.

The Miracle in Uganda

During the two days I was traveling to Africa, I didn't contact my sister. She didn't know I was on my way, although I told her I was coming home soon to see her and to lay hands on her. Those two days were bad for her, and by the time I landed in the country, she had taken a turn for the worse, and was seriously ill. My mother said she had become used to me praying for her. I heard that she was throwing her hands up in the air helplessly. People had already started to gather, waiting for her to breathe her last breath.

I landed in Uganda in the late afternoon and was asked by some saints to minister, spend the night, and fellowship with them. I agreed to that, since I didn't want to stay at my other sister's place, because she was still a Muslim. I called to inform her that I was in the country. She mentioned that Fatuma's condition had deteriorated, and was bad. I told her I would call her back, then I immediately called Fatuma. I was told she could not lift the phone, or even sit up. I told them to hold the phone to her ear, which they did. I began to pray in a heavenly tongue. I bound the spirit of death, and cast it out. Fatuma sat up, and we started talking like nothing had happened. I told her that I was in the country, and that I would see her the next day.

The next morning, I was supposed to meet my eldest sister to travel to my hometown. Instead, Fatuma was brought to the city that night, and admitted at Mengo Hospital. I went straight to the hospital with all my suitcases. When I arrived, Fatuma was breathing extremely fast, and sweating so much that the doctor would only allow one relative at a time at her bedside. I asked my unsaved sister to leave so that I could pray. I started praying in tongues and talking to Fatuma. The Holy Spirit took over. I could not stop praying. I was in emergency mode. I knew I looked different to them, I looked like a foreigner because I had been out of the country for more than eighteen years. They thought I was crazy, but her condition was not good, so I needed a manifestation of God's power. She needed divine intervention, and that's what she got.

She was on oxygen constantly because she could not breathe normally. Six nurses, who tried to take her blood could not find her veins, and gave up. I started praying in a heavenly language again when a nurse came in. I asked her to try once more to take Fatuma's blood. She agreed, and did manage to get a little blood, just enough to do a blood test. After a while, she came back saying she had to take another blood sample because the blood sample she took had become clotted.

Fatuma's feet were cold. She really needed divine intervention. We took turns cooling her body, as she sweated heavily non-stop. She had lost lots of body fluid, and was dehydrated. I anointed her with oil, and even had her drink a bit of the anointed olive oil. I was desperate! Perhaps that's why one day the Lord called me "Rhema Olive." I told you, I can be crazy at times, but it works all the time. I sang worship songs and read the Word to her; I bound and cast out the spirit of premature death; and I prayed. I was not going to give up on my sister. We grew up together, loved each other, and were like twins. No way, Death! *God has given us authority to exercise with every assignment.*

"Behold, I give unto you power to tread on serpents and scorpions, and over all the power of the enemy: and nothing shall by any means hurts you"
(Luke 10:19).

God always hears me, and in this case, He had given me, Rhema, a *rhema* word that He would heal her, so what was going on? In the natural, things did not look right. I told myself that weeping might endure for the night, but joy would come in the morning.

"For his anger endureth but a moment; in his favour is life: weeping may endure for the night, but joy comes in the morning" (Psalms 30:5).

"Pure religion and undefiled before God and the Father is this, to visit the fatherless and widows in their affliction, and to keep himself unspotted from the world" (James 1:27).

God is very concerned about the fatherless and widows Especially you!

I felt sorry for all the women, young and old, in that hospital ward with Fatuma. I cried, "Lord, not only my sister, but also these other helpless ones, I pray." In fact, one woman, who was taking care of her daughter asked me, "Are you going to pray only for your sister?"

"No mom," I said." I will pray for your daughter if you allow me."

I told her that I couldn't pray in the native language, I had to pray in English. She agreed and so I prayed for her daughter. The girl slept peacefully, and her mother was so grateful. She said her daughter had not slept through the night for a long time. The demons had her mind. She had been awake all night, hallucinating, and talking about all kinds of things when her mother asked me to pray for her. As I prayed for her, the girl resented this, objecting to the fact that I was always claiming the blood of Jesus. Of course, I knew that demons were the ones talking through her.

"And they overcame him by the blood of the Lamb, and by the word of their testimony; and they loved not their lives unto the death" (Revelation 12:11).

That verse excites me so much. I thought to myself, *it was Jesus' blood that conquered the devil on the cross; so, I will use the blood.* Seriously, I had not been using this powerful weapon as I'm supposed to, only in some circumstances when I was doing deliverance and encountered some stubborn demons. Friend, use the blood of Jesus; claim the blood of Jesus; His blood is forever powerful! This was the second time in a year I had been accused of using the power of the blood of Jesus in prayer. I have learned something since then about the power of His blood. Now I claim it, and let the blood of Jesus speak for me.

"And to Jesus the mediator of the new covenant, and to the blood of sprinkling, that <u>speaketh better things</u> than that of Abel" (Hebrews 12:24).

There was also a rich woman, also named Rhema, in that hospital. She was continually counting money. I asked her if I could pray for her because she coughed endlessly. She refused my offer for prayer that night because my sister had told her that though we both shared the same name, I was no longer Muslim. I felt sorry for her, but I wouldn't force my hands on her, though she watched me as if she wished I would offer to pray for her again. I did not pray for her, but honestly thought, *"Take your Muslim pride someplace else. I have been there before. One day you will bow to Jesus."* The next day she asked if I would pray for her. Of course, I did. The Lord intervened, and after I prayed, she slept like a baby; something she had not been able to do for a long time. My sisters and I could not help but laugh at her response to prayer. (Families are fun. Ours laughs a lot, and I miss those moments of fun, and real joyous laughter at times.)

Some of the women were asking for money to pay for their beds. You see, in Uganda, the hospital would not release them until they had paid their hospital bills. I suddenly realized there was more than sickness that needed to be addressed in the hospital. These families and patients didn't have the funds to meet their expenses. I asked the Lord to heal them quickly so they could go home instead of accumulating more debt.

Very early in the morning, I went outside to worship. Sleeping on the hospital floor wasn't pleasant anyway. On my way outside, I had a fascinating vision. Two angels were standing at the door waiting, and they would not leave until I got so mad in the spirit that I threw something that I had in my hand. That was in the vision. In the natural, I had nothing in my hand. Whatever I threw, hit the floor, and splashed like crystal glass breaking. At that point, the two angels disappeared. Where the crystal came from and what it was,

God only knows. Then I heard someone say, "You didn't have to call the emergency line."

I did not know anything about an "emergency line." Heaven has an "emergency line?" Absolutely! And we can dial it anytime. When one has an emergency in the United States or Canada, they dial "9-1-1." To reach heaven's "emergency line," you dial "3-3-3"—or Jeremiah 33:3! The Father invites us to call Him in case of emergency and He will show us great and mighty things. It was a wonderful revelation for me.

There is nothing new under the sun. Things become disclosed to us as we pray. The more we call on Him in prayer, the more revelation we will receive. He reveals His secrets to His servants as He says in Deuteronomy 29:29.

God is concerned about our knowledge. He wants to, and He is waiting to reveal great things to us. Call on Him! All true wisdom and understanding on earth originates from above, from the source, God Almighty. He chooses what and when to reveal things to us. After seeing the vision, I went outside and worshipped, prayed, prophesied, proclaimed, and decreed that the hospital beds would be empty on the third day. I said to the Lord, "Father, did you bring me here to bury my sister, and make me a reproach and a shame to my family? The shame will be on you as well. They will say that the God that Rhema serves has failed. They've heard that you have saved me, anointed me, and are using me."

The Lord answered, "Ask your sister to decide whether she wants to live, or to come home to be with me."

God is gracious. I knew then that Fatuma would not die, because God had given her a choice. I went back to the ward and found her sleeping. I told my eldest sister things were going to be bad unless God intervened, and she agreed with me. Fatuma opened her eyes. I greeted her by saying, "Praise the Lord!"

She answered, "Praise the Lord."

I told her "Fatuma, you have to be strong and fight. The Lord said you must decide whether you want to live, or go home to be with Him. The angels were already here, prepared to take you home to the Lord. Tell the Lord yourself that you want to live, and take care of your children."

She answered, "I want to live."

I led her in prayer to tell the Lord that she wanted to live and not die.

"I shall not die, but live, and declare the works of the LORD" (Psalms 118:17).

Shortly afterwards, two women and a young girl came into the ward, and went straight to my sister's bedside. Strange. I asked who they were, and they said they came from the church up the hill to pray for my sister. When they said "up the hill," I was reminded of Psalm 24:3.

"Who shall ascend into the hill of the Lord? Or who shall stand in his holy place? I will lift mine eyes unto the hills, from whence cometh my help. My help cometh from the Lord, which made heaven and earth" (Psalms 121:1-2).

That was our morning glory, it was an intervention we needed. Eventually, the Lord touched the entire ward. I asked the three early morning visitors if they were Christians. They said they were. I asked them if they were filled with the Holy Spirit. Again they said, "Yes."

Once I was satisfied about who they were, I asked if we could all pray for my sister in a heavenly language. When we finished, I asked them to ask the hospital nurse if we could pray for the rest of the sick people in the ward. The head nurse agreed. We became a team of four "Jesus nurses" who worked together with the Great Physician and Doctor, Jesus the healer. What could go wrong?

We began to pray for all who would allow us to pray. Some refused. One particular patient wanted us to pray for her, but her son refused because they were Muslims. What were we to do? We would not force anyone. The coming of these three saints opened the door for me to minister to the rest of the patients in the wards. By the third day, they would call me if their patients were suffering. I was referred to as "Jesus' ambassador." Which of course is true. Second Corinthians 5:20a says, *"Now then we are ambassadors for Christ..."* The nurses were there, but what could they do? In many cases, it was beyond their ability. They had to bring it to "Doctor Jesus." Let God be God.

That night, the ward was peaceful. There was no crying from pain, or groaning— no sadness. They only called for the nurses a few cases, and in those cases, the nurses said they would have to wait for the doctor to arrive in the morning. Where does our help come from?

"I will lift up mine eyes unto the hills, from whence cometh my help" (Psalms 121:1).

When the nurses took a nap, some of the relatives would come and ask if I would go to their family member's bed and pray. Joyfully, I would go with them. I would go and pray for the sick, most of the time singing worship songs to the Lord on their behalf, and the sick person would fall asleep; just as David played on his harp to King Saul and the evil spirit would depart.

On the third day, the doctor came and discharged literally everyone in the ward, except for the few who refused prayer. Lady Rhema was the first to be discharged. She was smiling and seemed very happy and grateful. My sister, Fatuma, remained, but was taken off oxygen. The doctor said she wanted to monitor her for one more day, and then she would be discharged. Fatuma was now talking and smiling, no longer panting and sweating. We suddenly had so many empty beds to sleep on, we joked about it, saying, "Just make sure a nurse doesn't come in the night and inject you!"

That was it. The next morning—like the resurrection morning—all was well. My eldest sister asked for prayer, as did Fatuma's sister-in-law, who is a very humble woman. They are all young widows. Sadly, there are very many widows in Uganda. It was hard for me, knowing that my eldest sister did not yet know the Lord, but God promised to heal them both. As I write this, I still pray for my eldest sister, and two of my brothers to be saved. The rest in our family are saved.

Praise the Lord for what happened in that hospital. Many were healed and discharged from the hospital on the third day. And to cap it off, Fatuma is healed and healthy. It has been eleven years now, and she is still alive, and it is well with her soul. She is a prosperous business woman, the best tailor in town! Praise the Lord!

God is concerned about everything, especially about healing us. He answers the prayers of the destitute, causes the rain to fall on the just and the unjust, and is a faithful God. After the hospital ordeal, I went and ministered at a church in my hometown. As I ministered, the demons began to manifest, and a few people began to scream and roll on the floor. The prayer team ministered deliverance to them, but there was one stubborn demon who resisted intensely. I went and whispered in the victim's ears, "The blood of Jesus is against you." Out it came, and the lady became calm and stopped rolling on the floor. There is power in His blood.

It's time for us to return to the basics. We have become so modernized that we have given room to demons. Let's do what Jesus did. When demons manifested, Jesus cast them out, there and then. There is no need for a person to make an appointment to see a counselor or pastor in two weeks. Was it because Jesus did not have an office, or an anointing that broke the yoke? Who does the anointing? God anointed Jesus of Nazareth and He went about teaching, healing the sick, and casting out demons.

Talk about travelling evangelists. Jesus did all that, so don't criticize the office of travelling evangelists. They don't work for you; they are doing the work of the Lord. (Romans 14:4) In the spirit, I have seen myself on an icy mountain, but I remain warm because on the mountain of God, He keeps you warm. Sometimes, I am like an eagle flying in the spirit. One day I related this to my spiritual mother in Holland and she unveiled some wisdom to me. I had a strong feeling that I was in Uganda, in person, even though I was still in Vancouver. Three days later, I was talking to my brother, Ben in Calgary, and he asked what I brought for him from Uganda? I asked him, "What do mean? I haven't been to Uganda."

He said, "People in Uganda said they saw you in Uganda."

Well! I reminded him that we had spoken a couple of days earlier that week, so how could I have been to Uganda and back so quickly. I called my sister in Lira and she said, "How come you didn't visit us?" I explained that those were just rumors. That is when my spiritual mother reminded me of the anointing on Philip, and his experience with the Ethiopian eunuch in Acts 8. My brother in Ontario was convinced that I was in Uganda. Yes, in the spirit I was in Uganda. This happened when the church was on a fast. Many things happen, and we receive great revelations when we fast and pray. Glory to God! Prayer works, and although it is true that it's hard to pray, press into prayer; and the Holy Spirit will come to energize you.

"The LORD upholds all who fall and lifts up all who are bowed down" (Psalms 145:14).

Never give up praying. Continue to get up for your prayer watch. Always advance; never retreat. Your miracle is on the way. Being ready in season and out of season means to always be prepared for each task He places before you.

"Verily, verily, I say unto you, He that believeth in me, the works that i do shall he do also; and greater works than these shall he do; because I go unto my Father" (John 14:12).

"17 And these signs shall follow them that believe; In my name shall they cast out devils; they shall speak with new tongues; 18 They shall take up serpents; and if they drink any deadly thing, it shall not hurt them; they shall lay hands on the sick, and they shall recover" (Mark 16:17-18).

"And to Jesus the mediator of the new covenant, and to the blood of sprinkling, that speaketh better things than that of Abel" (Hebrews 12:24).

"And they overcame him by the blood of the Lamb and the word of their testimony; and they loved not their lives unto the death" (Revelation 12:11).

CHAPTER TEN
GOD OF THE IMPOSSIBLE

I went home to see my dear mother before I returned to Canada, my peaceful nation. I was happy, knowing that my sisters would live to declare the mighty works of God. Amen. I can now sing joyfully…

> *"¹… I saw also the LORD sitting upon a throne, high and lifted up, and his train filled the temple. ² Above it stood the seraphims: each one had six wings; with twain he covered his face, and with twain he covered his feet, and with twain he did fly. ³ And one cried unto another, and said, Holy, holy, holy, is the LORD of hosts: the whole earth is full of his glory"*
> (Isaiah 6:1-3).

I have seen the hands of the Lord work the impossible. What is impossible with men, is possible with God. Our God is a great God. This is not all that the Lord has done for me; nor is it the only miracle He has done. I am grateful. Not only are my sisters healed, but I have them to laugh and talk with on the phone. We are united again, our family relationship has been restored. It was such a healing! With love, I prayed for the land of Uganda. I declared, decreed, proclaimed and prophesied over the nation, and now we see many things happening. Over and over again I say, "Thank You, Lord

Jesus, for your precious blood, for the cross; and thank You in advance for the great and mighty things You are yet to do. Thank you for everything, in Jesus' Name, Amen."

Recently on another visit to Uganda, I was blessed to see my sisters welcome me at the airport. We celebrated. None of them were sick, or coughing, or struggling with inflammation, or indigestion.

> "22 The Lord shall smite thee with a consumption, and with a fever, and with an inflammation, and with an extreme burning, and with the sword, and with blasting, and with mildew; and they shall pursue thee until thou perish." "59 Then the Lord will make thy plagues wonderful, and the plagues of thy seed, even great plagues, and of long continuance, and sore sicknesses, and of long continuance. 60 Moreover he will bring upon thee all the diseases of Egypt, which thou wast afraid of; and they shall cleave unto thee. 61 Also, every sickness, and every plague, which is not written in the book of this law, them will the Lord bring upon thee, until thou be destroyed. 62 And ye shall be left few in number, whereas ye were as the stars of heaven for multitude; because thou wouldest not obey the voice of the Lord thy God" (Deuteronomy 28:22, 59-62).

Once, while I was on a forty-day fast, the Lord helped me realize how powerful He is, from how He dealt with the plagues of the Egyptians.

"Come now, and let us reason together, saith the Lord. Though your sins be as scarlet, they shall be as white as snow; though they be red like crimson, they shall be as wool" (Isaiah 1:18).

So I used His Word, and said, "Lord, You are the God who put those plagues on the Egyptians, and the One who removed them. Even this AIDS plague is nothing to You. You are Almighty God. You can heal my sisters, and all glory will be given back to You." God understands. Yes, we must approach Him reverently, but He is always there to listen. He knows our hearts and our motives.

"For the word of God is quick, and powerful, and sharper than any two-edged sword, piercing even to the dividing asunder of soul and the spirit, and of the joints and marrow, and is a discerner of the thoughts and the intents of the heart" (Hebrews 4:12).

Bring the things that concern you to Him, and approach Him boldly. He will listen to you and give you what you want, for the Judge is your Father.

"⁴ For thou art not a God that hath pleasure in wickedness: neither shall evil dwell with thee. ⁵ The foolish shall not stand in thy sight: thou hatest all workers of iniquity" (Psalms 5:4-5).

"5 Thou shalt not bow down thyself to them, nor serve them: for I the Lord thy God am a jealous God, visiting the iniquity of the fathers upon the children unto the third and fourth generation of them that hate me; 6 And shewing mercy unto thousands of them that love me, and keep my commandments" (Exodus 20:5-6).

I repented for the sins of my family, all the way back to the third and fourth generations, and this act of faith and obedience broke the curses of those generations. Additionally, I asked the Lord to have mercy on my sisters, whose husbands had been sexually unfaithful, and I pled on behalf of the children who would be left without fathers or mothers. I reminded the Lord that I am His handmaiden, His jewel, and asked Him to move on their behalf for my sake. Remember, how the Lord did things for His friend Abraham; and for the sake of His servant David.

Are you a friend of God? I am. Yes, we are righteous in Christ Jesus. We have to know who we are in Him so we can boldly approach His throne, knowing that Jesus paid the price, and that His precious blood washes us white as snow. I reminded God of the covenant of the blood I have with Him in Jesus Christ, so He could not deny me the healing of my sisters, and the other women at the hospital. I stood in the gap, as an intercessor, and I would not let Him go. I reminded Him how merciful and loving He is. Trust me, it didn't come as easily as what you are reading now.

I remember sweating heavily in my bedroom as I labored in prayer and fasting. Though I knew the battle was won before I even set my foot in Africa, yet I continued to pray until I saw the manifestation of God's healing power. It was warfare!

You can't know someone has AIDS by simply looking. They do not advertise it, or as the lepers in the Bible, go about saying, "Unclean, unclean;" warning you to get out of the way so they can pass. Some are so wicked and deceived, that they want to spread the virus so that they will not die alone. Watch and pray. Seek the Lord for what he has in store for you. Don't just go out and get what is not yours; or take the risk of dying prematurely. Keep your body, the temple of the Holy Spirit, clean.

If and when the Lord wants you to marry, He will bring the right person into your life. He gives good gifts, so wait patiently on Him; though it won't always be easy. He will sustain you, and give you the grace to control your desires. In due season, He will bless you.

"The blessing of the LORD, maketh rich, and He addeth no sorrow with it" (Proverbs 10:22).

The Lord is gracious and compassionate. On my second visit to Uganda, my eldest sister took me to see an old family friend, and as we were coming back, she said, "Thank you for your prayers." I turned and looked at her, and she continued, "I went to the clinic, and my doctor was very happy that I'm taking my medication so well. He has tested me and there is no AIDS virus in my blood."

I said, "Glory to our God, who answers prayers!" What can you say? His Word testifies to it all.

> *"2 Bless the Lord, O my soul, and forget not all his benefits: 3 Who forgiveth all thine iniquities; who healeth all thy diseases; 4 Who redeemeth thy life from destruction; who crowneth thee with lovingkindness and tender mercies"*
> (Psalms 103:2-4).

He heals all our diseases. The power of my God is awesome. He is God of the impossible.

God is concerned about everything, especially things that are beyond our abilities.

This revelation was so strongly imparted to me that the Lord gave me a song to sing as a praise to Him for this miracle: *Beyond control, bring it to Jesus!*

CHAPTER ELEVEN
THE UNCHANGING GOD

God is the same yesterday, today and forever. He continues to do great and mighty things. On January 1999, at the World Evangelism Conference hosted by Morris Cerullo, God filled me with His Holy Spirit. At that point my prayer life went to a different level and direction; to a higher spiritual plane. I became a very excited Christian, full of power and authority, and much more. Am I satisfied? No! I want more of God. I want to see His face, to continue to be His glory carrier. Above all, I want to see souls won to His kingdom.

On one occasion, after putting my son to bed, I went into our bathroom. The bathtub was my prayer altar. I prayed and asked the Lord to show me His glory. I was determined to pray until the Lord revealed Himself to me. As I prayed, the Holy Spirit showed me my foot, and that I was wearing very high heeled silver metal boots. Then He asked, "What do you want?"

I understood that if I were to see the face of the Lord, I would not live. I was reminded how Enoch walked with God and was no more. After receiving this insight, I became satisfied with the revelation of my combat boots, so I thanked the Lord, got up and went to bed.

This is how I was baptized in the Holy Spirit at the conference. Nobody laid hands on me. I was praying in the hall before the afternoon service since I had access to the conference room before the meetings. I prayed, "Lord, like Jacob, I won't leave this place until you've baptized me with the power of your Holy Spirit."

This was close to the end of the conference. To make matters worse, I had sponsored a sister who I had met at a home meeting for women. She was an immigrant and mother of four children, so I paid for her roundtrip airfare to Anaheim, California. And she got baptized in the Holy Spirit that afternoon in the hotel room. Her husband had initially agreed that she could come to the conference, but he later changed his mind. But the Lord broke through all of that and she was able to come to the conference. As a result, she had received her blessing, and God was faithful and blessed me before the conference ended as well.

In November 1996, before I left Vancouver, the Lord gave me a vision. In this vision I was driving a vehicle in the snow. The Lord said, "Drive slowly, you will have to make a U-turn, but if you drive fast, you will get lost in the snow."

God is very concerned about where we live and how we live. When I returned to Vancouver, I rented an apartment near Kingsway and Dumfries, a major intersection. Then I invited a few brothers and sisters to come and pray and bless the apartment. One sister suggested that my place would be good for a Bible study, so we started a Bible study group. Later we added intercession as well.

The number of people attending increased and eventually became a church, which was called Calliope, which means "beautiful-voiced." Three of us were praying as we launched this church. There was Virgina, the pastor; Togo, and me. One day in my morning devotion, the Lord said, "My general."

I continued doing what I was doing, and He said again, "My general."

So, I wrote down what He said.

That evening, when the circle met, we prayed, fellowshipped, and shared what the Lord was saying and doing. I told them how the Lord had called me His general that morning. Pastor Virgina got very excited, in her American accent, she said, "Girl, do you know what that means?"

"No," I replied.

She advised me to read Cindy Jacob's book, *Possessing the Gates of the Enemy.* Cindy, the co-founder of Generals International, is a humble servant of God. The next morning I bought a copy of the book. When I got to the third chapter, I discovered that the title "General," in the context of God's kingdom, refers to the third level of intercession.

In 1999, I attended a Spiritual Warfare Conference in London, England, where I found myself in a prayer circle of mighty men and women of God all interceding for the conference, before the speaker, Dr. Morris Cerullo, came to minister. We were in a large circle with everyone holding hands, praying in unity. People! It pays to go to church or get to a conference early. If I had chosen not to go early to that meeting, I would never have met those prayer giants. Sister Marilyn Hickey was also there. I love how God uses her to reach the Muslims in a simple and profound way. She is fun

to watch, and hearing her share her testimony is very
encouraging.

CHAPTER TWELVE

CHILDREN DREAM AND HAVE VISIONS

One of my sisters has a cute little daughter named Susan, who looks like her late dad, Denis Alip. Susan is amazing. Even though she was only four years old when I first met her, we bonded right away, as if we were old friends.

While her mother was recovering at our eldest sister's house in the city, Susan was not allowed to go to the city to see her mother. When I saw Susan, I felt sorry for her because she missed her mother a lot. I spoke up on her behalf, and took her to the city with me to see her mother.

I would wake up early, before breakfast, to pray and do a prayer walk around my sister's house, before the Muslims started broadcasting their morning call to prayer. They use loudspeakers to do so, and the screeching sound of it is quite irritating. My sister's house is always a full house. She has so many people living there, everyone shares a room with a few other people. So, it is often quite noisy at daybreak. She has nieces and nephews who stay with her during the school year so they can get a better education; and during the holidays they travel back to their parents, or to their other relatives' houses. Sadly, most of them are orphans.

One morning after my prayer walk, I went into my sister's room. Little Susan was in there with her mother. She woke up and said, "Mommy, Jesus came in the night and brought us bread to eat." Oh! I was excited to hear a four-year-old testify about Jesus as the Bread of life.

"What else did Jesus do, Susan?" I asked.

"He gave us bread to eat," she answered.

I said, "Susan, Jesus came and gave you and your mother the bread of life, so that you could eat and live."

This is divine healing. The work of the Lord is visiting children, and confirming healing. Jesus, the Bread of life, took the bread and said, "If you eat my flesh, you'll live forever."

> *"28 And it shall come to pass afterward, that I will pour out my spirit upon all flesh; and your sons and your daughters shall prophesy, your old men shall dream dreams, your young men shall see visions: 29 And also upon the servants and upon the handmaids in those days will I pour out my spirit"* (Joel 2:28-29).

What more can I say, but praise my God for His goodness! He is so merciful. Susan loves to praise the Lord, and attend church. I was told that if anyone suggests missing church, she will say, "I am going to tell the pastor." So, her whole family dresses up and goes to church. Don't you love her already? You see, God is concerned about you and your family. I am amazed at how salvation is popping up in my family like popcorn. I enjoy watching to see the goodness of God.

"And if it seem evil unto you to serve the Lord, choose you this day whom ye will serve; whether the gods which your fathers served that were on the other side of the flood, or the gods of the Amorities, in whose land ye dwell; but as for me and my house, we will serve the Lord" (Joshua 24:15).

I was raised as a Muslim, so when I was saved, my family and friends rejected me. They couldn't understand why I had become a Christian. Many attributed it to the fact I was poor in spirit, and did not understand the Koran.

I was the first person in my family to become a Christian. For years afterward, I was an outcast. But I would tell Emmanuel, that God is with us. His right hand and holy fire constantly confirm that He is with us. With all humility, I can tell you that most of the time I literally feel His hot hands on my shoulders, and when things are bad, He comforts me, as if He is saying, "I am right here; not far away; right here."

"23 Am I only a God nearby," declares the Lord, "and not a God far away? 24 Who can hide in secret places so that I cannot see them?" declares the Lord. "Do not I fill heaven and earth?" declares the Lord" (Jeremiah 23:23).

With that revelation, I am strengthened and refreshed to move on until I receive a new assignment and another touch.

Perhaps you know what I am saying.

I have grown to trust the Lord with all my heart. He would never lie to me, because He loves me. He does not gossip about me, because He is my best friend. I can call upon Him, and He is here. He is my all-in-all, my everything. I love and adore Him, and no one can take Him from me, period! We are bonded, one for eternity.

When I was seven-years-old, I would follow older people to the well to fetch water with my little tin, so I could take a bath. In Uganda, we usually went to the well in groups, but this time I went alone. As I walked along, suddenly I heard a beautiful melody. I looked behind me, but there was nobody there. I looked all around, and didn't see a soul. Something told me to look up, and when I did I found myself gazing at the royal blue sky, and in the sky appeared two angels with golden trumpets. Without thinking I said, "I want to sing up there, too."

I heard a voice say clearly, "You are not ready."

I don't remember what happened next, but I do have that beautiful memory. In 1998, the Canada Post issued a postage stamp with two angels blowing golden trumpets. As soon as I saw the stamp, I remembered that open vision and I heard the Lord say, "You are ready!" Since that experience, I sing to the Lord and love on Him with sweet melody, and I mimic the sound of a trumpet with my bare hands.

When I was growing up, anytime I would have a dream I would tell my mother or whoever else who was around. I was always with my mother, and she took me everywhere she went. When my mother was admitted to the private hospital to give birth to her last-born, Oula, she took me along to take care of her, instead of any of the adults. Sometimes my mother would have severe headaches. When she did, she would call me and say, "Bring the oil and pour it on my head." I was young, and knowing nothing about anointing oil, I used cooking oil.

When my nieces and nephews were sick, she would ask me to stay home and nurse them while the others went to weed the gardens, and do the other chores. Many of those dreams have come true. Sometimes I will be in a place and say, "I have been here before." Then it clicks. The first time, it was only a dream or a vision, but now it is real.

Listen to the young ones, those little kids you think are so young. God speaks to them, and has assigned angels to guard them. So, listen to them and watch out what you do to them. God is concerned about them, too. Remember that before conception, God selects the womb into which he places each of them. God is a spirit. God's breath is life. That's why the Bible says we must fear Him who can not only kill the body, but can kill the spirit as well.

"And fear not them which kill the body, but are not able to kill the soul: but rather fear him which is able to destroy both soul and body in hell"
(Matthew 10:28).

You can abort a baby, but that does not mean you have destroyed everything. You have only killed the body, but the spirit of that child is beholding the Father's face in heaven. We will meet those children who've been aborted. Yes, there are so-called Christians who are no different from non-Christians. They kill and repent, committing all kinds of sinful acts, and excuse themselves by suggesting that we are in the age of grace. Yes, that is true, but what about the conviction of the Holy Spirit? Please don't abort your child. They are not hindrances, they are blessings who are meant to be born. And you have been chosen to be their mother. Thank God for the honor.

"God is a spirit: and they that worship Him must worship Him in spirit and in truth" (John 4:24).

Life is formed and DNA exists at the moment of conception. Do not think it is wisdom to take the morning after pills to destroy what is life in your womb. If you try to get rid of a life in your womb, consider yourself a murderer, plain and simple. It doesn't matter whether you were raped, or just having fun, be wise in all you do.

Let's return to the Lord, let's get back into His Word, the Bible. No fornication; no sex before marriage. Yes, the Lord can and will sustain you. Simply ask for His grace. God does not wink at, or ignore sin. Please do not kill, because that child in you bears the image of God. Call out to God, He will see you through. Like the song says, "Jesus loves the little children." Love them, because they will grow up fast. You will be amazed at what they turn out to be, great men and women of God. Wait until they start to preach to *you*, telling you all about Jesus. Just listen and give them all your attention.

"So God created man in his image, in the image of God created He Him; male and female created He them" (Genesis 1:27).

The Truth Speaks

God loves you. He is concerned about your life, both now and also after death, and He has provided a way for you to choose eternal life through Jesus. All other religions and religious systems that exclude Jesus will lead you to nothing but death. Christianity is truth. Can you imagine trying to talk to a god, who never answers you, for years? How do you know that your god even hears what you are saying, since he cannot communicate with you? Dummies don't speak and idols don't respond. They are dead, lifeless, so do not waste your time on religions that offer these lifeless, non-speaking gods. The God that I serve and know, through Jesus, speaks and answers prayer. He is Lord of my life and my best friend. He is a God who loves to relate to, and fellowship with His children.

Without Jesus Christ as your Lord and Savior, even though you are physically breathing now and believe that you are alive, according to God's Word, you are spiritually dead. You are dead in the sense that you have no relationship with your Maker. The only one who can reconcile you to Creator God is His Son, Jesus Christ. You may have been searching, and may have tried many things, followed different philosophies and religious teachings, but you still have not found the answer you are looking for. I understand, because I was also there, searching, just like you. Now that I have found the Truth, who is not information, but a person, I know that you too can find the Truth and have life abundant, eternal life. Jesus Christ is God's Truth!

God is concerned about you knowing the Truth

Do not be deceived, don't delay, call on Jesus now. Choose life and begin to enjoy eternal life. Being born again is sweet, yes, it really is; and full of fun. It is not boring and strewn with conflicts. However, the deceiver, the devil, knows you want to find out what the truth about God is, so he will keep trying to confuse you, and get you to move away from God. But, the Bible says that Jesus defeated him more than two thousand years ago, and anyone who receives Him as their Lord is more than a conqueror.

When you become a Christian, you will be engaged in this fight with the devil, as he tries to shift your attention away from God. Always remind him that he is defeated. He was crushed more than two thousand years ago when Jesus who died on the cross, rose the third day from the dead. It was on the cross that Jesus declared, "It is finished." Three days after that declaration, Jesus rose from the dead, and He lives forever.

Of all of history's religious leaders, Jesus Christ is the only one whose birth, life, death and resurrection was prophesied 600 years before He was born. Jesus Himself foretold His death and resurrection, and to fulfill the prophecy, He did die and was resurrected three days later. He is the only one who lives forever, conquering death. Believe in Him.

If you have not accepted Jesus as your Lord and Savior, do so. It is easy. For instance, we all know there are two sides of a coin—heads and tails. We all know the head is the best. In my mind, God the Creator is the head and the devil is the tail. So, if you have not yet accepted Jesus as your Savior, the one appointed by God as the only way to be reconciled to Him, you automatically belong on the other side, which is the tail, the devil; and he is nobody's friend. The devil is a deceiver, a liar, capable of giving you nothing but trouble, and eventually death. He is the ultimate loser, and those who follow him will share his eternal punishment.

Call on Jesus right now. Pray, "Father, in the Name of Jesus, forgive all my sins, come into my heart and be my Lord and Savior. Thank you. In Jesus Name, Amen." If you sincerely prayed that prayer, you automatically became a Christian. Now look for a Bible-believing church, tell the pastor what you just told God, get your own Bible and read it constantly. The Word of God is your daily bread. As you eat physical food to live physically, feed your soul with the Word of God. There is much to learn and discover in the Bible. Read the Bible, pray, worship the Lord, fellowship with other

Christians and you will live life abundantly. God is concerned about you making Jesus, Lord of your life and living in relationship with Him. In return, He will take care of you.

God is concerned about everything, especially about little babies, and you, especially you—yes you! To God be all glory!

God IS concerned.

He loves YOU so much.

Don't you ever forget!

God bless you.

www.ingramcontent.com/pod-product-compliance
Lightning Source LLC
Chambersburg PA
CBHW021827090426

42811CB00032B/2059/J